Thank you!

AA.

Money and Mental Wellbeing

by Dr Afiniki Akanet

Money and Mental Wellbeing
by Afiniki Akanet
© Afiniki Akanet 2022
Produced and published in 2022
by Affinity Global Enterprises (AGE) Ltd
www.afiniki.co.uk

Paperback ISBN: 978-1-7397416-2-4
Ebook ISBN: 978-1-7397416-1-7

Printed by TJ Books Limited, Padstow, Cornwall

Dedication

To my loving husband, Bolade, who patiently helped me see money differently. Even though we have different personalities and do not always agree, I thank God for bringing us together - "The result of which is a multiplication, not an addition".

To my wonderful children, Sophie and David - for motivating me to look after my money and mental health. Thank you for teaching me so much through our conversations and your curiosity.

Acknowledgements

I would like to appreciate everyone that contributed to the process of writing this book, including my friends and family (too many to mention) who rubbed minds with me on these topics, and have encouraged me over the years with my writing.

Thank you also to my publishing team, and people around the world that took part in my online survey in December 2021 and January 2022.

I hope you all get to read this book too.

I would also like to specially appreciate those who made time to review this book and gave valuable feedback before it was published. Thank you very much!

Mr Glenn Webb
Dr Bola Taiwo
Mrs Margaret Greenway
Dr Rupinder Kaler
Mr Matthew Ling

Contents

Part 1

Introduction

1.1 - What is money?

Money is a medium of exchange, usually circulating coins and banknotes, that can be used to pay for goods and services in present times. Money can also be described as a unit of account with which things are priced. For most people, money represents value. It is used to separate buying from selling, so I do not have to have something you want right now in order to exchange for something I need. Money saves us the hassle of trying to figure out how many bags of rice a car is worth! We no longer trade by barter because money is generally accepted for such exchange and gives purchasing power. Money is considered a principal measure of wealth.

It is often said that "money makes the world go round". As currency, physical money is circulated internationally to facilitate trade. Over the years, we have seen the value of the currency in different countries go up and down, influenced by several factors. Currency makes up a small amount of the overall money supply in an economy, especially in our increasingly cashless societies. The very wise and wealthy King Solomon is recorded to have said that "money answers everything". Money is one thing that affects us all, because we all have needs.

1.2 - What is mental wellbeing?

Mental wellbeing is about being in good mental health. The World Health Organisation (WHO) defines mental health as "a state of wellbeing in which an individual realises his/her own abilities, can cope with the normal stresses of life, can work productively and is able to make a contribution to his/her community". This is a state of wellbeing I expect most people want to be in. It is an integral part of health, because good health is a state of complete physical, *mental* and spiritual wellbeing. Mental health is actually more than the absence of mental disorders.

In England, one in four adults (and one in ten children) will experience mental illness each year. Mental health is influenced by socioeconomic, biological and environmental factors. Considering the recent impact of the Covid-19 pandemic on these factors, it makes sense to expect these figures to increase. Many of us will know someone who has experienced or is experiencing mental illness, such as anxiety, depression or psychosis. This makes mental health another topic that affects us all. Mental health is very important for our ability as humans to think, interact and enjoy life. This is why there have been many campaigns to promote looking after our mental health everyday - not just when there are diagnosed mental disorders. Mental health promotion is about actions that promote psychological wellbeing for all of us.

1.3 - How does money affect mental health?

Considering the significant part that money plays in our day-to-day lives, it is not hard to see that any problems in this area can affect our mental wellbeing. If money represents value and purchasing power for the things we need, we can imagine that people with less money might feel less empowered to do whatever they want. Persistent socio-economic pressures are a recognized risk to mental health. Socio-economic factors include income, education, occupation, wealth and where someone lives. Having access to the resources we need can be good for our mental health, whereas constant feelings of inadequacy, due to having too little (or *feeling* that we have too little), can have a negative impact on mental health, which is why a lot of health promotion measures target inequalities and poverty.

The term, "absolute poverty", is used to describe a condition where individuals do not have enough to maintain basic living standards (food, shelter, clothing), whereas "relative poverty" is about lacking enough to maintain a good standard of living compared to economic standards of living in the same area. A man riding a bicycle may be considered relatively rich in one area and relatively poor in another, but someone with no food to eat is absolutely poor by any standard. Although we may not know (many) people who are absolutely poor, there are several people who live quietly in relative poverty around us - people barely surviving from one payday to another, up to their necks in debt and worrying every day about what might happen if they lost their source of income.

Even having a lot of money has effects on mental health. People work hard to get to a place of financial freedom and comfort, but may be ridden with worry about losing it all. Some rich people might struggle to take time off work because they feel there is so much at stake, but they are then at risk of mental burn out - sleepless nights worrying about savings or loans, racing minds pondering on investments and endless meetings with accountants/managers. With more money comes more options and responsibilities. Some people also find security in their money/assets, which is why there is so much emotional attachment to wealth. The British Broadcasting Corporation (BBC) reported in 2014 that the economic crisis in Europe and North America led to more than 10,000 extra suicides in the recession! The report said that job losses, being in debt and home repossessions were the main risk factors.

1.4 - How does mental health affect money?

Being in good mental health can allow us to make better money decisions. We are able to think more clearly and avoid unnecessary risks. You may know of people who earn a lot of money but have nothing to show for it because of issues like alcoholism, gambling and mania. Some, who appear to have no addictions, also suffer poverty because of the lack of concentration and organisation to plan their finances and future well. They might keep high interest debts or spend so much on things we consider unnecessary, because of the state of their mental health. In fact, consistently having less than seven to eight hours of sleep per night was linked to taking more risky financial decisions in a study. Poor sleep is sometimes due to mental health problems, such as anxiety and depression, but we can also be sleep-deprived because of poor time management and stress. Sleep deprivation can then lead to poor concentration and irritability, which can affect our relationships and mental health eventually.

Being in good mental health allows us to perform better, which hopefully translates to more success at our jobs or businesses. Healthy people have more confidence to apply for promotions and ask for pay rises that can get them more of the money they want. When we feel good in ourselves, we can have better relationships to help grow our businesses and network for more opportunities. People like to associate with happy, successful people, which is why it sometimes seems that certain people have all the luck. Being in that state of mental wellbeing helps us to read other people's emotions better and become a favourite in places where stressed, grumpy or self-centred people have failed. Good mental health also helps people to be more resilient when they face challenges and disappointments.

Mental health is also important when it comes to money/finances, because it can affect our perception of problems. Someone in good mental health is better able to see a problem for what it really is, and think of sensible solutions or ask for help. When we feel overwhelmed, stressed, depressed or anxious, problems can appear bigger than they really are, leading to feelings of hopelessness and helplessness. This is why talking about our problems can be helpful, so that we can get someone else's perspective and advice, if possible. People sometimes struggle to open up and socialise when in poor mental health, making it more likely for them to make serious financial mistakes when trying to solve their problems in secret. Some get into unsafe levels of debt and expensive habits that make the situation worse, further damaging their mental health.

1.5 - Why this book?

I am a General Practitioner (family doctor) with a special interest in mental health. For years, money was not my favourite topic to discuss, but I had to face it - even through gritted teeth. Problems do not go away because we ignore them, so I had to learn to listen to people and read books by people who are "good with money", and reflect a lot on why I did not like talking about money. These reflections over the years, and my experience as a medical doctor, which gives me the privilege of hearing many other people's stories, have led me to write this book. I believe money and mental health are linked in more ways than we realise.

This book will be exploring the links, and how we can look after our mental health in this area. I understand that we all have different circumstances and prospects, but this book has fundamental principles that can be applied to any situation. I grew up in a middle class Nigerian family in West Africa, so my family was not wealthy - but certainly not poor. Coming to study in the UK as a teenager exposed me to financial challenges I had never experienced, but thankfully I managed to complete my medical education - with a lot of debt! Now I am blessed to be living a life I only imagined all those years ago, but I have learned so much about money and mental health through the process. I am still learning, but I hope that you will allow me the honour of sharing what I have learned with you in this book.

Most people want their children (or the next generation) to do better than they did, but we sometimes neglect to give them advice and explain the consequences of different options. This book will be sharing some of the money advice I wish I had *before* I started managing my own money. Our parents/guardians do their best with the knowledge and resources they have, but it is up to us to build on that to create better lives for ourselves as adults. It is not just genes and money that parents pass on to their children. Some of the habits and lifestyles we have are a reflection of what we saw growing up. The topics in this book might help us understand better why some people are the way they are about money and associated matters. It can also help us to see how it affects or is affected by mental health.

We were forced to reflect on our jobs and finances during the Covid-19 lockdown, especially in England where we had more than one. Certain jobs were described as "key worker" roles, which the nation could not do without, and meant plenty of work/income for those staff, even in a pandemic. Other roles were made redundant or remote, because of the changes necessary. I had patients that were out of work for months and struggled with anxiety around going back to work or retraining. Some people found amazing online business opportunities, courses and jobs in the lockdown which helped them keep mentally active and financially secure. My charity work and connections abroad also exposed me to people who suffered real poverty and threat to life in the pandemic. In 2020-21, there were young families experiencing financial and mental distress they never imagined.

In 2020, I reflected on the concept of opportunity cost, as regards to personal time and money, because both are finite. This is one economics lesson that has stuck with me since high school. Opportunity cost is 'the loss of other alternatives when one alternative is chosen". People had to really reflect on what was most important to them. Sadly, some people made decisions that were heavily focused on gaining more money - at the expense of their mental health. It is a well known saying that you cannot burn the candle at both ends, but it seems to me that with better internet and access to online resources, many people have tried to do just that by overstretching their time and money, without realising the impact on their mental health and family life. Unfortunately, such decisions have far reaching consequences, as we see more people experiencing domestic violence and adverse childhood experiences due to a rise in mental illness and home stress in these difficult times. Sadly, adverse childhood experiences and abuse have a tremendous impact on lifelong health and opportunity as well.

I am not sure how you feel when you read about suicide figures, but this is something we need to be preventing through mental health promotion. I feel this book is an avenue for us to reflect on our own financial habits and mental health, which are both very important, so that we can make any changes needed to reduce negative impacts on our health and those around us. Thankfully, most people reading this will not already have a diagnosed mental disorder, so I hope that it can be an eye-opener and motivation to protect our mental health and live intentionally when it comes to making/managing money. Sadly, many of those who really need to read this book might not make the time to do so or may be genuinely unable to (due to their life circumstances), but we can help them by passing on information, which is sometimes more valuable than money. The way we manage our finances now can determine our expectations for the future and options in old age. I am definitely not a money expert or a psychiatrist, but have spoken with several over the years to link these two important matters in a digestible format and help us make good choices to live the healthy, happy lives we desire.

Part 2
How We Make Money

2.1 - Background Factors

Most people think of getting a job as the main way to make money. The idea is to simply put in time and effort, in exchange for money and other benefits. Even teenagers can make money by doing small jobs, if they do not want to be completely reliant on adults to give them money for the things they want. You do not always need qualifications or references to get a job, because people can get paid for other skills or manual labour. People can also get paid for their ideas when they come up with solutions, creations (eg music, videos, gadgets) and business plans. Making money is usually about providing goods or services that people are willing to pay for.

If only it was that straightforward! There are several factors that affect our ability to get a job and make money. Even the teenager who wants to make money mowing neighbours' lawns, for example, has a few factors to consider. The area he lives in will need to be safe enough for him to move freely after school for such jobs. He needs to be fit and healthy himself for the work he plans to do. The neighbours will need to be trusting enough to grant him access to their homes, and they too will need to be trusted to make payment for services provided. Depending on how involved/caring his parents are, they will need to be satisfied that he will not be exposed to abusers and negative influences by doing this, and trust that he will be honest about how he makes and spends his money. His family's relationship with the neighbours could also affect his chances of getting such work from people; and their neighbours will need to be able to afford such extra expenses. We can already see that even before they turn 18, the earning prospect for children living in nicer, affluent areas is already better. We cannot choose where we are born, our health condition or who our parents are, but we can choose to make the best of what we have.

It has been known for years that household income plays a crucial role in determining a child's prospects. This is not to say that children from low income households or those with health challenges do not do well in school. Research shows that they start well but the educational attainment gap between children from lower and higher income families gets wider by the time children get to secondary school level, and this has sadly widened during the

Covid-19 pandemic. As they become adults, they then have to face competition in the big wide world when applying for jobs. The stress of living in poverty (and associated factors) will usually have led to poorer educational outcomes and less employment opportunities. These background factors can affect the kinds of jobs people feel confident to apply for and their ability to access internship opportunities.

People usually go into jobs and lifestyles they have been exposed to as children. There are few people that are brave enough to venture into fields unknown to their families, probably because we like to stick to the familiar. We will all have heard of an exceptional person who defied all odds to become the only professional in a blue-collar family, or the only successful business person in a family of doctors. It takes a good deal of resilience and mental wellbeing to go for the jobs/professions that we consider to be successful. Often, these background factors from our childhood and environment give us the advantage or disadvantage, even before we make our first university or job application.

Someone who is struggling with anxiety and self esteem issues will be less likely to apply for public facing or public speaking roles, no matter how well-paid they are. We see patients who struggle through life, changing almost every year from one job to another, because of their poor mental health. Their earning ability and chances of progression in companies is being affected by their mental state, which is sometimes as a result of childhood abuse or traumas, which were no fault of their own. Even people who had good childhood experiences and education might be limited in confidence, connections and earning prospects because of challenges affecting their mental health in adult life. This could be because of stress and illness from personal choices such as illegal drugs, unhealthy relationships/habits, excessive caring responsibilities and unmanageable debt. People can also struggle because "life happens" - bereavement, divorce, disability, war, physical illness etc.

There is no health without mental health. Even if people look physically healthy, if they do not feel well in their minds, they can be so limited in how much they can achieve financially, leading to different outcomes than we would expect for their lives. This is the big gap between *wanting* and *doing*. So many people want the top jobs and money, but are not able to do what it takes to get there, sometimes because of background factors affecting their mental health, or sheer laziness! While there are people with diagnosed mental health conditions who get help to achieve a lot in spite of their diagnoses, there are others who sadly do not realise the impact of their mental health on the career choices they are making and on their finances. There are many professionals and top business people who are taking antidepressants and antipsychotics to keep going, but it is sad to see that some people with even mild depression, anxiety, attention deficit disorder and personality disorders are not accepting the psychotherapy/medication/advice they can get to help their mental health, which is having an impact on their ability to earn the money and better lifestyle they desire.

2.2 - Vision and Motivation

How we make money is strongly influenced by our motivation and goals. The sad part is that many people are not intentional about their goals. Most young people want to be successful, but only those that set clear goals and work hard will get there. Some people boldly write down their financial goals, and it is no surprise that they achieve it - with hard work and patience. The famous actor, Jim Carrey, told Oprah Winfrey how he wrote a cheque of ten million dollars to himself "for acting services rendered" because that was his dream, and he actually made that amount of money for a movie he starred in years later. If we do not know where we are going, we won't know when we get there.

When it comes to making money, having a vision of the type of income, business, career or profession we want, helps us to focus our energy in the right direction. Having a focus makes it less likely for us to waste our time and resources on courses, investments, apprenticeships and jobs that do not contribute to our goal. When people are able to manage their resources and focus well, they achieve little successes that boost their morale as they journey towards their greater goal. Happy days make happy months and a happy life. Someone who has no focus or plan will find it difficult to enjoy their work or deal with challenges that may arise. This poor state of mental health then has a negative impact on their current role and leads to feelings of depression.

It is often said that "if you do what you love, you will never work a day in your life". This is the dream for most people - to be able to spend their days doing something they enjoy and get paid for it. This too is possible, with planning and perseverance. The journey might involve having to do some jobs you don't love before you get to the place where your hobby can pay the bills, but it takes determination to see this through. Some people are unable to make good decisions about their career paths, because they do not really know what they want/enjoy. They derive motivation from things like money, status or the approval of others. There is nothing wrong with finding motivation elsewhere, but it is worth understanding how such motivations might affect our mental health. Someone who is motivated by money may train hard for a well-paying job, in spite of the daily misery of the job, which might lead to depression and very little sense of accomplishment in the long run. Some professionals choose certain specialties or departments because of the greater financial reward, not because of interest. When they finally start making the money they hoped for, they might realise that there is no job satisfaction or fulfilment for them there. This might contribute to the midlife crisis that these people experience. People who want status may slave away for years in respected roles for very little financial reward, leading to financial stress and bitterness. Their families might even resent them for not being able to provide little luxuries, in spite of their big reputation in public. Some people whose personalities do not suit the high status, fame and/or leadership positions they go for might find life difficult in the public eye. We also see young people who endure university courses or jobs that they hate, just to win the approval of their parents or peers. We spend several of our waking hours at work, so you can imagine the negative impact this has on other aspects of our lives and mental health if we have to endure jobs/roles we hate for long periods of our lives. This internal conflict can sometimes manifest as anxiety, panic attacks, insomnia, depression, addictions or even physical health problems (somatisation).

For some people, the main motivation for work is financial need. Some people just work or run businesses to pay their bills. Some will be motivated by dependants or other interests that need financial support. Some people even have to leave the comfort of their home countries as economic migrants, because of the level of financial expectation their families place on them, which exceeds their earning power there. The income meant to maintain one home is relied on by three or more other families, including the worker's parents and siblings. This can often motivate people to work long stressful hours to be able to meet the demands of their extended family. Sadly, the risk of burnout is increased, because they are usually not able to switch off from their stressful lifestyle and do things that are good for their mental health. Holidays are considered a luxury due to never-ending family "needs". They cannot discuss their mental health issues or take time off because they feel that is a sign of weakness. People like this can sometimes present with hypertension, anxiety, insomnia or even heart attacks. Those who put financial pressure on themselves because of their own expensive taste can often burn out before they get to enjoy the large houses and flashy cars they work so hard to buy.

While some have motivation and strong drive, we also see people who have very little motivation for work. If they work, they will be content to do the same stagnant job for 40 years until retirement, if possible. Motivation is sometimes influenced by our exposure and mental state. If you grow up in an environment where nothing much is expected, it is easy to feel satisfied with less than your full potential. If you are surrounded by people who do not push themselves, it is hard to want to do so yourself. If you are clinically depressed or anxious, it is difficult to have the concentration or motivation to work harder. It is hard to think clearly and work on ideas for business or creativity when mentally unwell. When you have good days and ideas, the inability to raise capital to start a business or showcase your ideas can be frustrating and further damaging to mental health. This frustration becomes more pronounced when people wake up in mid-life to realise that their peers are doing much better than they are because of the work and thought they put in during their youth. Although most people are not motivated by money to do their jobs, they can become seriously demotivated by the lack of it.

Even people who seem to be doing well financially can run into mental problems when there is no motivation, purpose or satisfaction. National statistics figures for England show that high earners in professional jobs are more likely to be regular alcohol drinkers than those on average incomes. Young people and low earners tend to binge drink, but higher earners (who can afford it) tend to drink alcohol more regularly, often exceeding healthy limits. Alcohol is considered a socially acceptable way of relaxing, but it is actually the depressant some people are taking everyday, instead of dealing with the real issues. The stresses of everyday life in high-flying jobs and the need to keep up appearances can often lead to alcohol dependence and other addictions.

One Nigerian proverb translates as "work is the antidote to poverty". I believe poverty is not just a lack of money in this case. Whatever it is we lack, either because of gaps in our upbringing or disadvantages from our youth, we can work towards repairing it. We can learn new skills and unlearn bad habits to change our mindset, prospects and perspective. Working should never be all about making money. We build relationships, develop skills and get a sense of fulfilment by contributing to society through our work or business. Money is really just a means to an end. If your current role is not helping your mental health, it might be time to start looking around for something else. If paid work is not available, voluntary work can give you some of the benefits of work for your mental wellbeing, while improving your curriculum vitae (CV) for future job applications.

2.3 - Desire versus Reality

Most people want to be rich, or at least able to afford all the things they need. Even those that say they do not care about wealth can usually appreciate the good things money can buy. We might not care so much about material things, but it is nice to be able to pay bills and engage help without financial struggle. Money allows people the freedom to pay for services like cleaning, cooking, childcare, private healthcare, home help, private tuition, music lessons, accounting services, legal advice, travel, family experiences and holidays, if they wish. For many people, the desire for these things is mainly for their children or elderly parents, and not even for themselves. I still smile when I remember hearing someone say that, "Whoever said money can't buy happiness does not know where to shop!". People can become unhappy when they consistently have unmet needs, and no hope of improvement in their circumstances. This does not mean that having everything you want guarantees happiness either, which is why we are reflecting on the different ways that money affects mental health.

If the main way for making money is getting a job, how do people cope when there are not enough jobs for those wanting to work? How do they cope when they work hard but there is no room for progression? What happens when people are motivated to earn more and do better, but feel limited by the lack of business opportunities around them? What happens to their mental state when they see their peers getting opportunities they cannot access because of discrimination or victimisation? What if they feel that their background factors are preventing them from breaking out of poverty? With more access to the internet and social media these days, people can see others enjoying the things they desire, which would not have bothered them before when they were surrounded by only people in similar situations. There is more tendency for people to compare their lives with others and become desperate for money these days. Even though the link between poverty and crime is not always straightforward, it is sad that people living in long-term poverty have less access to resources and opportunity, and are more likely to offend. The effect of lack on people's emotional security has the strongest impact on criminal involvement. Government and Non Governmental Organisations often focus their poverty alleviation schemes on young families, pensioners and lone parents, which often leaves young single adults in more hardship with less help. These are often men living alone in despair because their desire for a better income does not match up to the reality they experience.

There is nothing wrong with wanting more when we accept the reality of the time and effort it will take to get there. The problem arises when people want it all - now! It is also problematic when we prioritise the need for more money over everything else. You might be familiar with the Bible quote, "The *love* of money is the root of all evil". Money itself is a good thing, but love for and desperation for money is what could lead people into making bad choices. When people focus so much on what they want, rather than what they already have, feelings of ingratitude, greed and envy start to creep in, which is not good for our mental health. People might end up losing priceless things like happy relationships, a good reputation and a clear conscience for the sake of money. Even people who seem to be doing well in good jobs can also fall prey to this, if not careful. When the desire for more money is so strong, even professionals and successful business people can be drawn into committing fraud (embezzlement, false representation, collusion, theft, misappropriation of funds and conspiracy). This is usually because of financial strain (e.g. due to debts, gambling, alcohol, drugs, dependants, bills) or to enhance their ego which they feel depends on how successful they appear. The relationship between fraud and mental illness has not been well researched, but there might be links to personality and impulse control disorders.

Most people who commit fraud will not have a mental illness. The three factors considered to be important for fraud to happen are motivation, opportunity and rationalisation. The motivation can be simply the desperate desire for more money, which is why it is helpful to reflect on this and curb it at this level. There might be genuine financial strains from debt and bills which act as motivation. This is why we will be discussing how our management of money can affect our mental health in part 3 of this book. The motivation (and reward) for fraud in some cases might not be obviously financial - people might feel pressured by peers or managers to meet business targets that are unrealistic for them. It is important to step back and regularly discuss such targets in organisations to reduce mental stress on workers that can lead to unwise decisions when *opportunity* arises. Opportunity refers to access to objects, software or money that makes the fraud possible. People then *rationalise* their fraudulent actions, weighing the pros and cons, telling themselves that fraud is okay, through a process of "neutralisation" which relies on cognitive distortions.

It is not fair that some people work all day and can never make more than they are currently making, while some people get to work less hours and make more money. It is not fair that some people get paid more for the same job in one country than in another. It is not fair that in some parts of the world, women still get paid less than men for the same job. It is not fair that some people get invited for interviews just at the sight of their surnames or university names, while others apply for years without getting one interview. There is so much that is unfair in the world we live in, but we need to decide for ourselves what we are willing to do or not do for the sake of making money. In a world where people are often judged by their appearance or what they can afford, we need to balance our expectations and conscience depending on our own background factors, prospects and level of motivation. There is no need to keep resenting the person who studied for years at university to get a higher paying job, when you did not or were not willing to put in the work yourself for such training. There is no need to envy the stay-at-home mum as she spends time with her children in the park when you are not willing to give up your expensive car and nice office. When we take time to balance our desires with realistic expectations, we can make better choices that will be good for our mental health. If it means accepting things you cannot change, or making uncomfortable changes for success, we will be more likely to enjoy better mental health in the long run. Some people have had to take a pay cut, emigrate, go back to school, go to rehab, seek medical help, start up or close down businesses, move house and even give up some professions to find the happiness they desire. If we continue to do the same things, we cannot expect to get different outcomes. If we are ready to make changes, in spite of any background disadvantages we might have, then we can expect results with time and perseverance.

While crime can seem like a quick and easy way of making money to some, the mental strain that comes with it is not worth it. Some have ventured into drug dealing, sex work and cyber crime as a quick way of making lots of money, sometimes to fund expensive habits/lifestyles, but criminals will often be looking over their shoulders for the police and are more likely to suffer anxiety, depression and even post traumatic stress disorder. Not to mention the risk of ending up in jail or dead! Almost half of adults in prison have anxiety or depression, and life after prison can be even more difficult as people struggle to integrate back into society. It might be hard to push yourself into financial freedom by legal means in the current climate - with funding cuts and the impact of Covid-19, but it is important to remember that life is not a race. Every successful person has their stories of failure. What we do not want is to set unrealistic financial expectations for ourselves and burn out mentally before we get there. Pacing ourselves with achievable goals and a grateful attitude is good for our mental health. Unfortunately, some people have done this all their lives and ended up with unexpected outcomes due to no fault of their own, but the peace of mind from a clear conscience is priceless. We see people who have ended up with a less than expected retirement life or unfortunate loss of their assets due to being victims of crime/corruption, natural disasters, unfavourable government policies or unstable economies. This can be a significant blow to one's mental health, but having supportive family/friends and other interests outside of making money can help people maintain their mental health even through these challenges. We will be discussing more on how to look after our mental health in part 5 of this book.

2.4 - Social Welfare

Social welfare refers to assistance programmes designed to assist and ensure the wellbeing of a nation's disadvantaged citizens. The commonly known welfare programmes in the UK relate to financial help for jobseekers, low earners, disability, housing, some parents, pensioners and carers. This is often referred to as "Benefits". Benefits are usually paid directly to the recipient's bank account from the government every two to four weeks. There are assessments that need to be made to determine if people are eligible for benefits. Some people find the process stressful and sometimes humiliating. Most people do not want to be in need of benefits, but find themselves having to rely on this for short periods of time till they get back on their feet. Others have to depend on benefits for years, and can often find changes to criteria or re-assessments very stressful. The government has limited resources and has to ensure that only people that really need these funds are getting them, but this sometimes requires confirmation from medical records and means testing, which I have seen people get really frustrated about. When people are used to living on a certain amount of income from benefits, they can get very anxious about government proposals for cuts to their income and changes to eligibility criteria.

Some people receive benefits because of mental health problems that do not allow them to work. Unfortunately, this also means that they sometimes struggle to manage their finances and can get into problems with managing their bills and debts. There are organisations and charities that help people with making benefits applications and sorting financial issues affecting their mental health, but people sometimes struggle to know when they need help or how to ask for it. People receiving mental health crisis treatment may be eligible for a debt respite scheme when a debt adviser applies to the Insolvency Service on their behalf for some "breathing space" where creditors cannot contact them about their debt for the duration of their treatment and for a few weeks after. Some people have felt very overwhelmed and even suicidal because of financial pressure from creditors, so this is a useful way to support people in mental distress. There is also breathing space of up to two months available in the UK for those who are not receiving treatment from an approved mental health professional.

People on benefits can also get help with other expenses, such as prescription costs, in the UK. Even though care from the National Health Service (NHS) is free at the point of use, each medication prescribed for most adult outpatients will normally need to be paid for. If people are struggling with their finances, this can deter them from getting the help they need. Exemption certificates and prescription prepayment certificates can help reduce this burden. As medical doctors, we sometimes have to do free prescriptions for relatively cheap non-prescription medicines like paracetamol and antihistamines because parents cannot afford to buy this for their children. The negative mental impact on a parent feeling unable to provide such little things for their own children can add up to them feeling depressed. Some parents become excessively anxious about their children's health and turn into "frequent attenders" to health services, while some feel too embarrassed to get help until the child ends up at the hospital emergency department with a worse illness. Some people might feel unworthy of any good thing because of the stigma around receiving benefits in some places. They might become withdrawn or aggressive because of their poor mental health, and this is sometimes taken out on the healthcare workers and receptionists they speak to. They might also feel bad about the life choices they feel forced to make because of their low income, and struggle to have confidence to access services. Some may feel judged by professionals who try their best to be non-judgemental, leading to patients ignoring signs of significant health problems such as those linked to smoking, alcohol excess, obesity and drug use, which they feel guilty about.

For people who have always been on benefits, it can be difficult to even consider going back to "normal employment", even when their condition improves. This is because change is difficult. They have spent years getting monthly payments without having to work, and it can be hard to manage the logistics of working around other interests and commitments, such as childcare. Sadly, some even advise their children to report having anxiety/depression and apply for state benefits as soon as they turn 16, because they do not understand the benefits of work. Even though some people think it is bliss to not have to work, we know that unemployment has negative consequences on mental health, such as depression, anxiety and low self-esteem. On the other hand, good mental health is a key influence on employability and staying in work. In January 2021, during the Covid-19 pandemic, it was reported that 43% of unemployed people had poor mental health, compared to 27% for people in employment. Furloughing had some protection for mental health, because only 34% of those furloughed reported poor mental health. The social welfare system aims to relieve the financial pressure from unemployment, but cannot provide the self esteem and mental health benefits people can gain from work when they are able to. It can be hard to get back into work, but there are many free training programmes available for those on benefits in England. Doctors can support people with fit notes to encourage employers to consider a phased return, amended duties or reduced hours initially.

Sadly, social welfare is not great in every country. It is helpful for the mental health of workers in more developed countries to know that they will get some government aid if they were to lose their jobs or ability to work. Life is very different for those living in poorer countries or countries with less care for disadvantaged groups. People work hard everyday in spite of the challenges and poor infrastructure, knowing also that there is no government safety net if things go wrong. Unfortunately, things are also more likely to go wrong in such countries because of poor health screening programmes, poor security and bad roads. Family units have to work together to look after each other. The mental stress of regularly begging from relatives and accepting irregular handouts is not good for people's self image and financial planning. Even elderly people almost have to beg for their pension entitlements after years of service. You often find that there is a lot of pressure on the breadwinners and young people in such societies because there is inadequate social welfare.

The financial strain can sometimes lead people into a life of crime and corruption. Even when there is support from the government or charity organisations, the mental health and dignity of those receiving it is not taken into consideration. They often have to queue publicly for food bags or vouchers, that might not even last a week! This leads to even more frustration and bitterness, especially if people really have no other option. We often get people from such countries ending up as economic migrants, refugees or asylum seekers in other countries, because of very poor conditions or disasters at home.

The mental health of refugees and asylum seekers is usually more fragile because of the trauma they may have experienced before leaving their familiar environment to a strange place. Some might have been respected professionals or business people who now have to rely on a low income from benefits in another country, sometimes with a different language. The culture shock and steep learning curves are all things they have to deal with while navigating how to manage their finances and get back on their feet. They sometimes have to deal with racism, discrimination and unstable housing circumstances in a new country, which people might not complain about when they are just grateful to be alive! The stress might motivate some to work harder to get out of poverty, but some will unfortunately suffer with Post Traumatic Stress Disorder, clinical depression, insomnia and panic attacks which can be debilitating, and keep them on benefits for several years. Children of these migrants may experience neglect and abuse because of their parents' mental health struggles, poverty and lack of strong social networks in a new country, possibly leading to mental health problems in the children which can present also as personality disorders and adjustment disorders in adulthood.

The response to the Covid-19 pandemic during 2021 was also worryingly unequal across the world because some countries could afford to give their citizens two to three vaccines, while others could not even afford one per citizen. Lockdown was difficult to enforce in poorer countries because people had to go out and fend for themselves without good social welfare systems. There was news of corruption relating to people hoarding and refusing to hand out international aid (food packages) in some countries. The feeling that a nation itself does not care enough for its citizens is not helpful for people's mental health, and can lead to an increase in antisocial behaviour and mental health disorders, especially if this is the only source of income/provision people have hope for.

2.5 - Passive Income

Passive income refers to income that is not attached to hourly wages or an annual salary. It continues to generate revenue after the initial work is completed. Some define it as income that requires minimal labour to earn and maintain, but you will find that a lot of time, money and energy is usually required *initially* to create a source of passive income. Passive income refers to income such as from stocks, royalties, rental properties or patent rights. People can also earn money from dividends as company shareholders and interest from transactions. Winning the lottery is a potential source of effortless income that many dream of - even those that do not play the lottery sometimes fantasise about winning the lottery one day! Some people are active gamblers and sometimes win money that way. The main problem with any kind of gambling is the risk of addiction, debt and huge financial losses over time. Gambling addiction has destroyed so many lives and homes, but there is help available, such as through cognitive behavioural therapy, national gambling helpline and gamcare (which supports loved ones of gamblers). Premium bonds provide another avenue for winning money without the risk of losing the amount put in, although no interest is earned over time and the value of money put in might be negatively affected by inflation.

Real passive income is when your money generates more money. Since we have limited hours in the day and not everyone will be able to enjoy working into their 70s, it is wise to think about ways of diversifying our income and creating sources of passive income which will come in handy when we might not have the energy or motivation to earn a wage/salary. Passive income is usually good for mental health because it allows people to have more free time to do things they enjoy, rest or spend time with friends/family. People with passive income can also be less stressed about changes to their work circumstances because they do not *need* their jobs to survive. It is worth speaking to a good accountant about the tax implications of certain passive income ideas, and working out what is best for you financially.

Passive income can also allow people the freedom to live wherever they want, if they do not have to go to work everyday. If we manage our finances wisely, and have no large debt repayments or bills holding us back, we can enjoy financial freedom even before the official/national retirement age. Passive income is not about being lazy, but about being smart with money. We can invest now to set up ideas, shares and properties that keep bringing in money with less effort in future. Sometimes, things do not work out as planned and we have to be more involved

than expected, but there will still usually be more autonomy than you would have as an employee, which is good
for your mental health. The problem arises when people
are easily destabilised by unexpected issues or do not have
an exit strategy they are happy with. Someone who cannot cope with uncertainty or unexpected issues like
tenant problems, complaints, legal matters and sudden
changes in legislature might find it more stressful managing their sources of passive income. It might be better for
their mental health to avoid such responsibility and stick
to regular employment without the stresses of management. This is not to say that we can't challenge ourselves
to function out of our comfort zone with support from
others. It is helpful to have a good exit strategy e.g. selling
your properties/shares or an exit clause from a contract/
partnership that does not leave you worse off, in case
things turn out worse than expected. There is no point in
carrying on with a passive income idea if it is causing you
more stress and affecting your mental health negatively.

Because many people still prefer the routine of 9-5 work,
it can get lonely if you are lucky enough to sort out
enough passive income to quit employment. There might
be no one to sit at the beach with when everyone else is at
work on a Thursday morning. Or you will find that those
who are not working might have no money to come

along! You might also miss the social interaction and daily challenges of working life. Although, Dolly Parton says in her song, Working 9 to 5, that "*They just use your mind, and they never give you credit. It's enough to drive you crazy if you let it*". Having more free time is only good for your mental health, if you know how to spend the time productively. As discussed above, going to work should not just be about the money. You might be able to find a good balance working for yourself and working for/with others. You might also have specific hobbies, like travelling or painting, that you can enjoy alone. If you decide to stay in employment or do not have passive income options at the moment, the important thing is to not let work "drive you crazy", as Dolly puts it. We will discuss more about looking after your mental health in Part 5.

If you have managed to save and invest to create or maintain solid passive income streams, well done! It takes a lot of financial planning and discipline to do this. People often dream of get-rich-quick schemes because no one likes the hard work part of making money. The truth is that the journey itself teaches us what we need to maintain our status. We hear of people who win or inherit large sums of money falling back into poverty/bankruptcy within months because they have not learned how to manage money wisely. People wonder about rich people who spend cautiously and poor people who spend frivolously, but this is usually the reason why they stay rich and poor respectively. We will discuss more about how we spend money in the next part of this book. It is a privilege to be able to manage our finances well enough to leave an inheritance for the next generation, which some wise young people might invest in creating passive income for themselves. It is just a shame though when we see young people living lazy lives because of their hopes of an inheritance. If people do not have a good work ethic, even the biggest inheritance can be squandered in just a few years. Having passive income can allow us more time to think and come up with great ideas and solutions to problems around us. Time to think is a luxury some people do not have when they are so mentally exhausted in a full time job. Some of the ideas we might come up with in our free time can even translate to more income, if executed well.

Volunteering is another great way to spend your time if you are blessed to have passive income. So many charities are struggling to get volunteers these days. Working in such organisations can let us see how other people live, give us the joy of helping out and make our days more productive. There is no compulsory time commitment when volunteering and you get the benefits of social interaction, even outside paid employment. There are also highly skilled voluntary roles e.g. charity trustees, treasurers, mentoring, overseas project managers or school governors that will be much appreciated if you have the time and skills to contribute to your community in that way.

People sometimes assume that famous entertainers and social media influencers are making passive income, but the reality is that they work hard to keep producing relevant content regularly to stay afloat - which is alright if someone is blogging or making videos on topics they feel passionate about. You can imagine the misery if someone had to regularly produce content on a topic they do not enjoy, just because they thought that it might be an easy way to make money. Sometimes lack of inspiration or "writer's block" can be a sign that we need to review the impact of our work on our mental health and make some changes. Simple tips like getting enough sleep, setting realistic deadlines/expectations that reduce pressure, sorting other personal issues that may be weighing us down and talking to others in the field can restart creative juices for those whose passive income is about creativity and royalties. If your passive income idea is not what you expected, it is never too late to change course, if necessary, for the sake of your mental health. So many famous people "go quiet" for some time and reinvent themselves successfully.

This is much better than carrying on, at full speed with poor mental health, until you have a mental breakdown.

As much as leaving or getting an inheritance can be a good thing, we need to be aware of pitfalls for mental wellbeing. It is wise to write a will for peace of mind that your wishes are known and can be respected. There have been so many family fall outs following the distribution of assets/funds after inheritance tax has been paid, where applicable. It is helpful to maintain a positive perspective when it comes to receiving such gifts. The difference between feeling bitter or grateful is often as simple as knowing where we are on the entitlement scale. When people over-commit financially in expectation of an inheritance, they can often be very disappointed when the total inheritance does not work out to how much they were expecting. Happy relationships and memories end up being tainted because of money issues. It is always better to live within your means, be prepared to work hard for yourself, and be grateful for whatever extra comes as an inheritance, which can be used for something more specific, like investments or projects. Interestingly, most millionaires never received an inheritance to start with!

The best thing about passive income is the free time and mental space that comes with it. If what we define as passive income is turning out to be bad for our mental health, it is worth looking at other sources of income that do not lead to chronic stress. A little stress can be good and exciting, but chronic stress can lead to depression, anxiety, addiction and even physical health problems. I know some landlords enjoy the "stress" of managing their own properties and buying/selling houses. Just because real estate is a popular investment idea these days does not mean that it is good for you. It is important to think about your own personality and what you enjoy doing. Think about easier ways of getting the same things done, e.g. hiring workers, estate agents, project managers, brokers or accountants who can help with managing complex tax issues. We sometimes see people who carry on with businesses because it is all their family has known and they do not want to disappoint people. They might be better off in other fields, but they carry on with no exit strategy. Eventually, they lose zeal for life and might even end up losing all they worked hard for. Remember, there is no health without mental health - health is wealth! If passive income is helping your mental health, remember that it is a luxury not many enjoy, and consider how you can use your free time to help others, because that will also boost your life satisfaction and self worth.

2.6 - Job Perks

The benefits of working are not limited to the wages/salary/dividends received at the end of an agreed period of time. Having a regular source of income can make it easier to prove your eligibility for credit, such as mortgages and loans. People sometimes confuse this eligibility for wealth, but it is important to remember that debt has to be re-paid. Just because the bank says you are eligible to borrow a million pounds does not mean that you should. It is still a debt that has to be repaid - no matter how low the interest rate is. Appreciate eligibility for borrowing as a perk of your current earning power, but remember that the money is not yet earned. Debt can be used as a helpful tool to buy property or make sensible investments, but can easily become a trap if not handled with care.

Even though people might be able to make more money from certain locum/casual or self-employed roles, some people choose salaried jobs because they prefer to have a steady income, with additional benefits like paid annual leave, sick pay, parental leave pay and in-house training. Locum or casual work is not for everyone. If you are not very motivated to seek work regularly from different places to keep up your income to cover your bills, you might find it stressful having an unpredictable working pattern or income. You also need to have the organisational skills to ensure invoices and payments are not missed when you work as a locum or supply staff, although locum agencies can help with managing some of these administrative aspects. There is also the tendency to overwork yourself when there is plenty of work available, in order to make up for periods of the year when there is less demand for your services. People who are not very good at managing their money and planning ahead can live in constant worry (without a steady source of income), even when earning a lot of money on paper. For those who can organise their finances and time well, the opportunity to earn more per day and work less rigid hours is a bonus of doing casual work or locums. This is often a great option for those who want to spend more time with their families or on other projects.

During the Covid-19 pandemic lockdown, certain groups of people were advised to 'shield' at home because of medical conditions that made them more vulnerable to serious illness from an infection. Many people had to isolate for ten days at times. One of the benefits of having certain types of salaried jobs was that people did not have to worry about their income being affected. They could still expect a salary at the end of the month when shielding or off with sickness. There might be time limits to how long companies will pay for sick leave, but knowing that an unfortunate incident like illness will not also lead to poverty has been good for people's mental health. People are able to concentrate more on their health, than on getting back quickly to work when they have such benefits. Some insurance companies offer income protection for those without such work benefits, e.g. self-employed business people or locums. It is worth doing the maths to see if the extra money earned from locum work is still worth it after paying personally for insurance and other time off.

Locums and casual workers will usually not get paid if they are off sick or on parental (maternity/paternity) leave. This can sometimes make people carry on working through sickness or stressful periods, such as soon after having a baby or bereavement. Unfortunately, some people who prefer to have salaried roles have not been able to secure good jobs. They had even more anxiety in the pandemic because they were not mentally or financially prepared for all the changes and lack of work. Some low paid workers were not able to work from home or get alternative income in lockdown, which led many families into financial difficulty. Even with the government support that was available in some countries, many families felt the financial impact, which was not good for their mental health. The cumulative effect of such stresses can often lead to feelings of hopelessness and depression. If someone was worried about sick relatives, unable to work for weeks, living alone because of a marriage breakdown, scared of getting ill themselves and struggling to pay their bills, for example, the constant worry can lead to poor sleep and appetite, which has a negative effect on how they perceive even smaller issues like not being able to get a doctor's appointment on the same day, and sadly lead to even more mental health decline, especially for someone with a significant past psychiatric history.

People who had regular income secretly admitted to enjoying the lockdown and having more time at home while getting paid. They were able to work on home improvements they never had time for, and catch up on phone calls with relatives, which was all good for their mental health. Even though spending more time at home meant more gas and electricity bills, people with a steady income did not mind because they were spending less on going out anyway, with non-essential services closed. It was a good opportunity for families to bond, but sadly led to more domestic violence and marital breakups for some because of other factors. Sharing the same home space for work and schooling everyday was unhelpful for some problematic family relationships. UK family law firms saw a doubling in divorce enquiries during the pandemic. Financial pressures were thought to be a contributor. Having a big house or salary does not guarantee happiness. Even people with regular income struggled for other reasons, as well as financial, if they were overstretched. We will discuss more about spending in the next part of this book.

Being able to take paid maternity or paternity leave after having or adopting a baby is a perk of paid employment. Some people have had to sacrifice their careers because of lack of support for parents in their professions. In most countries, women can take three to twelve months off after having a baby, even though a full salary is not always paid for the whole period. It can be helpful for working women's mental health to know that they do not need to worry about having no money while readjusting to life with a new baby. Where the income starts to decline after a few weeks, some women may decide to resume work sooner than they would prefer because they cannot afford to be without their full salary for too long, especially if they were high earners. 1 in 10 women will experience postnatal depression in the first year after giving birth. New fathers can also get depressed in the first year. This is different from "baby blues", which does not last for more than two weeks. For some people, going back to work after a few months and having more adult interaction is good for their mental health, but if someone is genuinely struggling with their baby or mental health, it is sad to think that they might feel pressured to go back to work for financial reasons when they are not mentally ready. It is not always about getting prescription tablets and carrying on, sometimes we just need time off to heal and recover after certain things, because we are human.

Presenteeism refers to situations where people come to work without being productive, usually because of ill health. Although some jobs offer perks like paid annual leave and sick leave, there can sometimes be stigma around taking time off with stress or mental health problems, so people continue to go to work when they really need time off. Sometimes staff shortages and company needs can make people feel guilty about having time off that they are entitled to. In this case, they are not working for more money, and are probably not seeing more results by being at work, but they could be harming their mental health in the process. On the other hand, we see people who seem to enjoy the "sick role" and frequently take time off work with "stress", especially if they get paid sick leave. Some take months off work and later struggle to go back to their normal routine when paid leave expires, because of new anxiety from not being at work for a long time. It starts to affect their self esteem and leads to other mental health issues, which can be truly debilitating. Workplace managers can often help by organising "back to work interviews" and "keeping in touch" days to support people back into normal functioning after having time off for maternity or sick leave, for example.

Another perk of good jobs is the prospect of having a decent pension after retirement. There is also a state pension available to those above official retirement age. It is fair that people who have worked hard should not have to suffer in later life when they can no longer work as they used to. Hopefully, they will also have less expenses at that stage, with mortgages paid off, so that a reasonable pension does not have to be a huge monthly payment. People can also pay into private pension schemes as an investment into their future, for peace of mind. There have been several changes to pension schemes, even for large organisations, due to scarcity of resources, but pensions are still a good idea, if you can have one. Some people even overpay into their pension schemes while working, as an investment for a better future. It is so sad to see older people worrying about money or living in poverty. Financial lack in old age can often lead to poor diet, vitamin deficiencies, unkempt appearance, lack of home heating in cold countries, unsuitable living conditions due to lack of home maintenance, reduced social interaction with peers, isolation, loneliness and consequently, poor mental and physical health. Some of the choices we make regarding work and pensions now will affect our lifestyle and health in future, so we need to think ahead, not just for the moment.

Reflection

- What factors from your past (or background) might have affected your current (or last) job/career choice?
- What is your main source of income at the moment?
- Do you have any other sources of income?
- What are the pros and cons of your current source(s) of income or job?
- Looking at the bigger picture, are there any changes you feel motivated to make for the sake of your mental health and future?

Part 3
How We Spend Money

3.1 - Bills and Basics

It is common sense to cater for our basic needs first when we have money. There is no point in buying expensive perfume with your wage, when you do not have food or clothing. Some people get into a misguided relationship with money when they start earning while living with their parents, for example. If parents are providing for their basic needs, so they do not have to pay for food, clothes, transportation or accommodation, they can really struggle to know how to prioritise funds when they finally move out of their parents' home. People get into adulthood not realising that you need to budget and pay for things like electricity, gas, council tax and rent/mortgage. They end up getting into financial difficulties, debt and stress, due to poor management of money; and some run back home to become a burden to their retired parents, or keep struggling for the rest of their lives, if they do not change. It sometimes seems mean or stingy when parents teach their children about these things by making them set aside money for basic bills from their first jobs, but people who learn to budget for basic needs will usually be more sensible with money as adults, and avoid unnecessary debt.

Paying for essential things like food, accommodation and utilities first will spare people the anxiety for these daily needs, and the embarrassment of always asking for loans or handouts due to poor financial planning. If you are blessed to have an income, no matter how small, planning your outgoings to fit around that income will save a lot of stress. When people live beyond their means, with regular bills that add up to greater than their income, it is no surprise that they will have chronic stress and will always complain of lack, even when they look rich. The regular feelings of inadequacy continue to chip at their pride and self worth, compared to someone who makes lifestyle choices that are conveniently covered by his/her income. This is the reason why people soon start to hate their jobs and feel frustrated, because they feel that they need more money, when what they really need is better budgeting of what they make, no matter how little or how much.

The definition of essential spending is influenced by several factors, including where we live and what we do. We all need food, accommodation and clothing, but some people

have to cover regular costs such as car maintenance, professional memberships, indemnity/insurance, internet access
and other services that some might not consider essential.
It seems that the more money people make, their basic bills
can easily go up to match their status. It does not always
have to be so. We need to be intentional in what we allow
to become an essential bill in our lives, so that we do not
become slaves to work. If your basic bills every month
amount to thousands of pounds, which you struggle to
earn, there will always be money-related stress in your life,
which is not good for your mental health. If your essential
bills are kept manageable, then you can have wriggle room
to work as much or as little as you want, depending on
your circumstances. People can choose to work part-time
or not at all, in order to spend more time with family at
different stages, if they are not over-committed financially.
The type of city, area or house we live in can also affect the
amount of money we pay for rent, council tax, transportation and other bills. When we realise the connection
between these choices, we can be more intentional about
how much financial pressure we want to take on. There is
nothing wrong with wanting better, if you can afford it.
What is really sad, is when people keep striving fruitlessly
to come out of financial difficulty without realising that
certain lifestyle choices, such as big houses, expensive cities,
brand new cars, an overactive social life and number of

children/dependants, have tied them to greater financial commitments that are leading to the chronic stress and anxiety they experience.

Some money decisions may have been sensible at a time, but it is worth reflecting from time to time to decide if changes are required to reduce stress. Sometimes the changes required might mean spending more to reduce other types of stress, which means that your basic bills might go up, but as long as you are intentional and can afford it, it will be good for your mental health. Some people decide to take on regular help with childcare, gardening, cleaning or bookkeeping. Others might decide to take on subscriptions for entertainment services, journals or club memberships. It is important to realise when making such decisions that money is finite. Unless you are earning more, and want to increase your basic bills, something else will have to give. We often see people adding on TV subscriptions, club/gym memberships, phone and car payments that they struggle to keep up with, because it seemed a good bargain at the time. Once the contract has been signed, it becomes a basic bill that has to be paid regularly. If you cannot really afford it, this opens the door to overdrafts, begging and borrowing, leading to more financial stress - on a regular basis. People not being responsible with their basic bills can also cause stress for people that care about them and strain on relationships, as we will see in part 4 of this book. The impact of unpaid bills and late payments on one's credit rating can also lead to limited opportunities, stagnancy and mental stress in the future.

Sometimes life changes can cause us to drop some bills and add on others. A home carer for an elderly relative, for example, might become a need if no one else is able to care for them in the family. There is sometimes support from the government's adult social care department in situations like this, but it usually ends up costing the individual or family some money, which may not have been planned for. This is another reason for keeping our essential bills lower than the maximum possible, so that we have some allowance to save for unexpected issues, and have less financial stress when problems arise. During the lockdowns of 2020, many of us realised that a lot of the things we consider to be essential were not really that important. If we could manage without eating out, holidays abroad, beauty treatments and cinemas for some time when they were closed down, we can be intentional about how much we spend on these things when there are no restrictions. The pandemic reminded us that we are all human, and what we really need is life, love and health. Some of the things we consider to be essential, might be mainly because we consider them helpful for a more convenient life and to boost our mental health after doing busy jobs, but we need to be sensible about how we commit to those on our direct debits, to avoid mental stress in case our circumstances change.

A laptop that might have been considered a luxury for a child was suddenly considered essential for homeschooling in the UK when schools were closed in lockdown. Mums realised they can survive without salons and spas, so those are definitely not basic needs. Dads could survive without pubs and football. Even though Netflix, Amazon and Sky might have saved us from boredom, they are also not essential to life. Some child in a poor country elsewhere is struggling to get an education, using a candle light to read books because of power cuts and lack of internet. When it comes to mental health, having a lot of money can be just as stressful as having no money, because you have more options and responsibility with more money. Being clear about what our basic needs and bills are is helpful for budgeting and better money management to reduce stress and mental illness.

3.2 - Dreams and Wants

Most of our spending in modern society goes on things we *want*, not need. We need few things to live, but human desire can almost never be satisfied. When we get what we want, we often think of something else we want. Even when we think we are happy, we see adverts everywhere trying to sell us things we don't need. If we have not learned to say no, or accept that we cannot have every-thing our eyes desire, we carry on in an endless pursuit of material things - more, more, more! Some of the things we want are desires from years ago that we are finally in a position to achieve, while others are momentary whims that might change in a few months. One minute people want a mansion, the next they want a house that is cosy and easy to maintain. One minute they want the latest electric car, the next they want to be able to afford the lat-est fashion. The thing about money is that choosing one thing often means giving up another option. Some people are wealthy enough to have many options available to them, which means that the more money people have, the more of their personality we can see. Their dreams and desires are not just in their heads, but also in their pur-chases. It is said that money makes you more of what you are. If you were a generous/caring person, having more money gives you the opportunity to do more of that. If you were a selfish/greedy person, having more money lets you exhibit more of that. How we make decisions with little amounts of money when it comes to things we want, is very likely to be how we will make decisions regarding wants when we have even more money.

"Retail therapy" refers to the idea of shopping to improve the buyer's mood. It is thought that comfort buys help to improve mood because of the restoration of personal control through shopping choices, especially when people feel sad that life is not going their way. Unfortunately, this happiness that comes from shopping comes at a cost and is short-lived. Some people have gone into huge amounts of debt trying to keep up with the happiness they feel from shopping. Some people might have compulsive buying disorder, which is an impulse control disorder related to personality disorders. Most people will not actually have a disorder or an addiction to shopping, but can shop for things they do not need to relieve feelings of anxiety or depression. Window shopping can give some of the benefits of retail therapy, without the damage to your bank account. Walking around shops and interacting with people, which means getting dressed and getting out of your house for window shopping, might contribute to these benefits. The feel-good effects of shopping start in our brains during visualisation, even before a purchase is made. With the rise in online shopping options, many people are doing the exact opposite by staying in bed and spending more online for even smaller benefits to their general health. There are options for same day delivery, buy-now-pay-later and credit card borrowing offering instant gratification, even when we cannot afford things. Waiting for purchased items to arrive by post might add to the excitement of online shopping, but there is even more excitement after patiently saving up for items we want - which is usually a better option long term. Everyone enjoys a bit of retail therapy from time to time, but if shopping is preoccupying your thoughts and causing financial problems, it might have become an addiction that needs to be dealt with.

People with mental health problems are three times more likely than the general population to have fallen victim to online scams, especially with the rise in internet shopping in the Covid-19 pandemic. Online scams often prey on our wants and fears. People were more likely to fall for scams related to masks, testing kits and Covid-19 cures in the pandemic. Reduced concentration and impaired decision making when people are not in good mental health makes it more likely for them to fall for scams, which can lead to more financial stress and mental distress. Even when people are not mentally distressed, they can sometimes be blinded by the strong desire to get something, that they miss small warning signs. It is always better to take more time to think about something before making a financial commitment, than to enter bank details or sign contracts impulsively. Even if something looks like a good bargain, there will usually be another sale or offer soon, if you do not get it today.

Being able to dream and achieve is actually good for our mental health. We can make goals and feel good about making progress when we achieve them. The excitement on the face of a couple when they finally buy their dream house or get that dream wedding says it all. It is good to plan ahead and work towards our goals, so that we are not just being impulsive or pressured by others to spend money in a way that puts us into financial difficulty in future. For long term projects like building a house, starting a business or paying tuition fees for a course, it is worth considering the bigger picture before you start. It is really sad when children and young people have to keep worrying about tuition fees because of poor financial planning by their parents or guardians. The stress from recurrent bills that one cannot really afford can be bad for the mental health of both parents and children. Some people never really recover from the trauma of the financial strain, which could have been prevented, because these are *wants* and not needs. We will discuss more about handling such decisions in part 5 of this book.

Recognising that something is a want, rather than a need also helps us to put things in perspective, especially if we cannot really afford it. This is not to say that we should not push ourselves to work hard for the things we want. As long as it is not to the detriment of our mental health, having big, achievable goals is great. Some people feel happiest when they are able to host parties, fly first class, send their children to the best private schools, have the latest technology gadgets and invest in every new idea, but it is important to realise that these are not needs. If you will have to get into unmanageable debt or suffer panic attacks while worrying about payments, it is not worth it. It may be worth thinking about the real motive behind these wants and dealing with that first.

Some of the choices we make are more to make us look and feel good. Being able to pay for our children's weddings or buy them the latest toys, being able to take our parents on holiday or show them our new car, being able to wear the best clothes and have fabulous hair every week - it is all good fun, until it is not. There are other ways to be happy and show love that do not involve spending huge amounts of money. If mental health is a priority for us, we will try to make money decisions that do not end up causing us more stress down the line. If we are blessed to be able to comfortably afford these things, while saving for the future, that's great. We can enjoy them with no guilt, because money does give us the option to do these things and be happier. The things we want are there to make life more enjoyable and convenient. Having access to a lot of money comes with a lot of responsibility. Even when we can afford any pleasure or thrill, we still need to be mindful of "pleasures" that can be harmful in the long run. So many people have destroyed their own lives and that of others through illicit drugs, gambling and other excesses. Too much of anything is not good.

Conditions like Bipolar Affective Disorder can cause people in mania to overspend and have grandiose ideas. It is important to be aware of early warning signs, if you (or people you live with) have a mental health condition that might affect spending habits. You can also set up safeguards through your bank, such as spending limits and text alerts. Even people who do not have diagnosed mental health conditions can sometimes struggle to control their spending, so these safeguards are useful prompts to stop us when we are going past our budgets. People can sometimes feel anxious or depressed about not being able to keep up with current trends or what their peers are doing. They might feel pressured to have big birthday parties, club memberships, private tuition, travel abroad, eat out or carry out home improvements they cannot really afford. It is always better to deal with the root cause of your feelings, than to keep spending carelessly. Sometimes, on the balance, you might be able to justify taking a loan to get some things you want now, as an investment, to protect your mental wellbeing or to have the ability to keep working, but it is never wise to take on more than you can afford, because the financial stress will harm your mental health eventually. Independent financial advisers and charities can help you budget and decide on affordability, if you are not sure. Affordability measures by creditors or vendors, e.g. house or car sellers, can sometimes be biassed, because they want to make profit from your purchase or debt. Progress starts with being realistic about our wants and earnings, and being honest with ourselves and our advisers.

3.3 - Savings and Investments

The purpose of investment is to make profit. You can invest time, money, effort or another asset with the aim of getting an increase in value over time. Most people think about business transactions when we talk about investments, but it is also important to realise that anything you do to improve yourself is also an investment, if done wisely. People spend significant amounts of money on furthering their education, getting specific skills or certifications and doing training courses, which can open doors for greater earning potential and opportunities. The time and effort invested in such training is also considerable, for valuable courses. People might take out loans for tuition fees for themselves or their children. There might even be government supported student loans available. The issue with such investments in people is that there are no guarantees. We see people graduating from university after spending tens of thousands of pounds on tuition and living expenses, only to choose a totally unrelated lifestyle or career, that may or may not have anything to do with the years of study and money spent at university. Others carry on with the qualifications gained to build successful careers and businesses that could have never been possible without that initial investment in their education. Some manage to build fantastic careers and businesses without university degrees (and cost), and choose to get qualifications in future when they can afford it and are sure what they need.

Whatever path you have chosen educationally, there is no reason to live unhappy or in regret. Change is possible when we reflect and are willing to make the effort to see a difference. Some people chose higher education courses that did not suit their personalities because of poor careers guidance during high school, and now continue in jobs they hate because of the guilt they might feel about leaving their careers after investing so much time and money. They might even feel guilty because of sacrifices made by their families to help them along the way. Others have left good career paths because of flashy ideas that seemed better years ago, and now struggle with the shame of having to go back to start from the bottom when their colleagues have made so much career progress in that field. Very few are lucky to have chosen well in their youth, invested the time and money for their career choice, and still enjoy the fruits of that labour. We are ever-changing as humans, and if a career change is what is best for your mental health and happiness at this time, it is better to overcome any guilt, shame, fear or regret, and go for it. All the experience adds up to make you better for your next role. Some people have been brave enough to weather storms and start new businesses or careers in midlife. Although making such an investment for education and self improvement has no guarantees, because life circumstances and desires might change, it is worth considering the value for one's mental health. If you are considering investing in courses and training mainly because of the monetary gain, take a moment to balance that with how helpful or detrimental that option will be for your happiness. You might make a lot of money but lose other priceless things. You might also make a lot of money for a defined period, have a successful exit strategy and enjoy profits from that investment for the rest of your life. The best scenario would be to make the investment and enjoy the gains for a long time to come, with no regrets.

In some countries, parents consider investing in their children's education as a retirement plan. This is especially prevalent in the poorer circles. Parents struggle for years to pay for their children's university education and later expect them to provide all their needs in future. The problem with this idea is that most people in their 30s are still trying to get on their feet financially. It would be burdensome to be catering for extended family needs while starting your own family and career. The mental health issues these young people face are not openly discussed, because they are just expected to keep working harder to 'look after' their parents and adult siblings, in some cases. This perpetuates circles of poverty because the whole family depends on one or two young graduates to sort out any family expenses, so the young people never get a chance to save or invest for the future. It is sad because this pattern continues for generations in some countries, usually because there is no student financial aid or reliable government support for pensioners. It is a mentality that can be carried along with such people into their diaspora communities even when they move abroad. I remember feeling sad for a baby when I heard his mother telling him he would be the one to buy her a car in future. With at least a 30-year head start, why is it impossible for this mum to envision buying a nice car for herself and also for her son when he is an adult? This poverty mentality often prevents people from seeing better possibilities, so generations of poverty continue when people do not realise they can be aiming higher and doing better. In countries where there are student loans and government financial aid, some parents kindly choose to invest in their children's education and save them the stress of taking huge loans as young adults. This is a great thing for parents to be able to do for their children, but can also lead to major financial and relationship strain if there was not good enough planning by the parents to be able to comfortably afford this and retire well. It might be wiser for such parents to have supported their children to go for more affordable study options, and for the parents to make other more secure investments for their own future, which will also help them to need less financial support from the graduates when the parents retire. People who invest wisely in their working years can be in a better financial position to support their adult children/grandchildren when they start having young families and buying their own homes. Those investments might pay off as good passive income for future generations.

While most of us know the benefits of saving, it is not always easy to do so, when we have so many expenses and limited income. We have all heard the advice to save for a rainy day, but some people live life from one "rainy day" to another, because they never seem to have enough money. The stress of living like that can be detrimental to mental health. Instead of repeating the same cycle every month, it might be worth writing down our income, expenses and usual "rainy day" problems, to see where the real issue is. Financial advisers, Citizens Advice Bureau and charities like Christians Against Poverty can help with this. It is always wise to have a budget, so that we know where our money is going. Saving happens when we include an amount for this (no matter how small) in our budget, and put it out of sight (possibly in a separate bank account). It is easier to save when we put it away first, not after all other needs and wants are met, because there will never be enough then. Someone who saves £10 a week, can easily have £500 at the end of the year to do something reasonable. Even though it takes a lot of discipline to save (sometimes even denying ourselves instant gratification and things we think we need), the benefits are great. The peace of mind, from a mental health point of view, of knowing that you have something put aside for emergencies, makes those unexpected problems less stressful. Obviously, the amount we need to set aside for emergencies will need to be proportional to the amount we make and the lifestyle we live. The purchases, projects and investments we can achieve with larger amounts of money saved over time can be more useful for our future than little treats regularly.

People who have proactive financial strategies tend to be happier and more satisfied with their lives. In an American survey, reduced consumption (more saving) was associated with decreased psychological distress and increased personal wellbeing. This was also true for students who usually manage money on a smaller budget. Financial success does not happen by chance, we need to consistently make choices that lead to financial freedom and prosperity. It takes time to change spending habits/mindsets and to learn self control with money, but the positive effect on our mental health and the environment is worth the effort. Saving is not about being selfish or greedy, it is about paying yourself before you pay everyone else. When you make £1,000 and spend it all on tax, food, bills, clothes and entertainment, what have you got left for yourself? What will happen if you need £100 next month and there is a delay in your salary being paid? Some people are blessed enough to be able to have savings to keep them going for years, even if they never get paid again. It is not about luck, they will often have saved intentionally by denying themselves some things and making sensible work and/or financial decisions. People who save are better placed to take up good investment opportunities and make even more money when opportunity knocks.

Property investments have become very popular in the UK. People can make money from rental income or property sales as the property value rises. Mental health should also be considered when making a choice of investment. Some investments are more stressful or risky than others. There are investment platforms and experts who can advise on stocks and shares, so that you do not have to go in blindly and lose your hard-earned money carelessly. Some might choose to invest in business ideas, using their savings as capital. Equity gained from property investments and dividends from other investments can also be used as capital. It can be very distressing and depressing to lose a lot of money in a bad business deal. This makes some people extra cautious and even averse to investments. There is always an element of risk in investment, but we need to make sure that we are in the right mental state for making such decisions. Even something as simple as having continuous periods of sleep deprivation can make people more likely to take riskier or poor financial decisions that can end up in a loss. This can then lead to depression, anxiety and financial stress. We can sometimes be emotionally driven when making investments, because of certain personalities or life experiences. Considering our feelings and mental health when investing is not always a bad thing, but cannot be the main motivation for making financial decisions, if we are to avoid pitfalls and ruin. People have found it helpful to diversify and invest mainly in areas of their own expertise, to reduce risk, anxiety and stress.

If your main investment is a business you run, it helps to take a step back regularly and look at the big picture. Investment in this way should not only be about making money. You can make decisions and run things in a way that is better for your mental health, even if it means making a bit less money. You also have the opportunity to be an employer and provide solutions as an entrepreneur. Focusing solely on the money can be detrimental to your mental health and that of those working with you. Some people have even lost friends and happiness, because of greed and selfishness in business. Your success should not depend on the downfall or humiliation of others. There is often greater success when people cooperate and business leaders look out for the interest of their teams. So many companies are now investing in the mental wellbeing of their staff because they realise that they get the best out of them this way. When staff are happy and thriving, they will give their best and the company will do better. You can also invest in staff training to give them a sense of progression and belonging, especially when they have shown commitment to the organisation. The Bible says in the book of Proverbs that he who oppresses the poor to make wealth will eventually end up in poverty. Ensuring people's wellbeing while building wealth and making investments means that we are also ensuring that we have a clear conscience and honourable motives in the process. There is nothing wrong with making profit and wealth, but pay staff fair wages in a timely manner and do not treat people badly, even if you think you can get away with it. Employees have their own problems too, and just because you are not making all the money you think you want does not make it okay to stress people who might not even have enough for their basic needs. Persistent feelings of guilt, conflict, shame and self-centeredness are not helpful for your mental health as the boss.

It is also very important to think long term when making investments. Making financial decisions just based on how we feel at the moment might feel good now, but may be detrimental in the long run. We see people who invest all their money buying property or businesses in their hometowns, for example, due to emotional attachments, but they end up struggling in retirement because of poor resale value or depreciation. If you are spending as an investment, it is always wise to do proper research and beware of your emotions. Some people also struggle financially because they did not realise the difference between assets and liabilities when spending. As an example, the value of brand new cars will usually depreciate and land will usually appreciate. Some good-looking investments can turn out to be liabilities and sources of stress, if not properly researched. Some people have bought properties that needed more maintenance and legal costs than expected, causing the buyer more stress and losses. Some people who cannot cope with such risks are better off paying for experts or staying away from certain types of investment, for health reasons. Even though there is always risk to be aware of, it is still advisable to consider savings and investments as a way of reducing financial and mental stress in the future.

3.4 - Tithe and Giving

Christmas is a season for giving, especially in the western world where we can spend thousands of pounds on Christmas presents for loved ones. We derive joy from seeing the faces of people we care about when they get something they like. Most times, people do not actually need the presents, but it is the thought that counts, as we say. Unfortunately, some people go crazy with Christmas giving and celebrations at the end of each year, driving themselves deeper and deeper into debt they cannot manage. The depression that follows in January is not only down to the dull, cold weather, but also because of the financial stress as they await another pay day which never seems to come soon enough. It is also possible that spending time with family at Christmas makes people more aware of their loneliness in January when all the celebrations are over. Of course, for someone with clinical depression, this deep sadness is not only limited to the month of January or "blue Monday". Everyone can experience feelings of depression and anxiety, but we can protect our mental health by reducing factors that contribute to this. From a money perspective, we can prepare in advance for the extra expenses of Christmas and stay within our budget with celebrations and presents, even if it means going for cheaper options or cutting down the list of those we give cards or presents to. If the main issue in January is loneliness, we can invest more time and money during the year to build better relationships and a more active social life, which will be good for our mental health.

People sometimes feel pressure to give more than they can afford. While giving is a good thing to do, especially when there are people in need around us, we should still think about our priorities and realise that resources are limited. If you give to every single charity that contacts you, you might end up having no money to pay for your own house. If you give to every cause that makes sense, without ensuring your basic needs and responsibilities are sorted first, you will end up begging and borrowing too. There are so many psychological benefits of giving, but it needs to be with wisdom and without compulsion. Giving makes us feel happy, reduces stress and encourages social connection. If we cannot afford to give lots of money, we can give our time and energy, which also gives us the benefits of giving without the financial stress. Volunteering our time also gives us a sense of belonging and connection to others, reducing stress and loneliness. This is a form of giving that gives back, because skills gained through volunteering can help to advance your career and provide job opportunities.

For the sake of our mental health, it is important to beware of developing a 'God complex' or 'saviour mentality' in our giving. You might genuinely enjoy giving and sacrificing for others, but it should not be because you have the grandiose idea that people or projects will not survive without you. This way of thinking can add so much pressure and stress to the giver, so that a good thing turns into a problematic issue for your mental health. It is healthier to consider yourself a channel for giving, rather than someone's ultimate source of provision. If, for some reason, you did not exist anymore, did you know that the need will be met in another way? Even people who keep asking you for money, as if they cannot live without you, will find someone else to ask, if you stop responding to every demand they make. Sometimes, people prey on the kindness and generosity of others, taking advantage for years, and never moving on from a parasitic financial relationship, if allowed. Even family members can sometimes display this 'entitled' attitude, especially when the giver feels like their 'saviour' and bends over backwards, even to his/her own health and financial detriment, to meet their demands. We will discuss more about how money affects relationships in the next section of this book.

Charitable giving is also a big part of many religious teachings, such as in Sikhism, Christianity and Islam.

Christians will usually give ten percent of their income regularly as a tithe, in obedience and gratitude to God. This involves selflessness, sacrifice and deeper spirituality, especially because it does not depend on how rich or poor one is. For people who believe in tithing, you will find that you can always afford it, if you pay it *first*. Then you can enjoy the rest of your money with peace and blessing, because what really matters is your budget (of whatever amount) and knowing how to stick to it. He who is faithful with little will be faithful with much, as the Bible says. If giving in this way is important to you, you can start even with the smallest income. Evidence has shown that spirituality and religious involvement are associated with better health outcomes, including greater longevity and better coping skills; less depression, anxiety and suicide. Even though people who tithe are living on less than 90% of their income, after tax and other giving/offerings, they can be happier and healthier because of their faith and discipline. Wealth for such people does not come by holding tightly to every penny, it is seen as a divine blessing.

Most faiths encourage giving to the poor and helping the needy. Even people of no faith see the moral good in giving to the needy, or helping friends/family. There is joy in giving, but we must be mindful not to get too carried away with giving, that we end up giving what we cannot afford, especially when there are basic bills and needs yet unmet. It is helpful to have a budget for our charitable giving, if this is something we wish to do regularly. Including this in your budget reduces impulsive giving from money that was meant for other very important needs or projects. Having a budget gives us freedom to spend without guilt. If you truly do not have money left over for giving to others after accounting for your own bills, you can say no to monetary requests without feeling guilty about spending money on yourself. This can also be applied in situations where young professionals feel obligated to give money to family members regularly, especially in black communities. If there are needs you really want to help with, you can intentionally factor 'giving' into your budget, so that you know what your maximum contribution can be, no matter how much pressure or emotional blackmail you might be getting. There might be negative responses from the family when you set these boundaries and become intentional with your finances, but it will pay off in the long run when you have less financial/mental stress and are able to invest in a better future, so you do not all end up in poverty.

People also give money with ulterior motives, such as for bribery and corruption. It appears as generosity, but usually comes with strings attached. This is a popular scenario in corrupt countries where people usually have to grease palms to get anything done in life and business. Access to public services, good jobs and government permits can be affected by bribery and corruption. It is difficult to budget in such societies because you never know when a bribe will be needed, even for the simplest service or business transaction. It then becomes a vicious cycle where those being bribed cannot live within their income because of regular 'tips' they are now used to getting, and those giving the bribes need to engage in more dishonest activities to keep making easy money that they can give away everywhere to have their way. People taking part in such activities often have to ignore their consciences to carry on with such dishonest living, but have to live in constant fear of the law and the possible consequences of their lifestyle. One study from Vietnam showed that even exposure to day to day petty corruption had a significant negative effect on mental health and reduced trust in local institutions.

Truly charitable giving is a great way to spend money, when we can afford it. It has psychological benefits for the joyful giver and grateful receiver. As humans, we will always have bigger dreams and desires, so giving is not something to postpone until we have all we want. There will always be others who have much less than us, and will be grateful even for the crumbs from our tables. Giving is a matter of the heart, sometimes even a matter of sacrifice. We can choose to have one less bottle of wine or one less holiday to be able to make a difference to someone else by our giving. We can also choose to give our time and energy, if we really do not have money to give. When we work hard, manage our finances wisely and reduce mental stress from financial problems, we can build wealth and be in good mental health to do more for others in need.

3.5 - Insurance and Healthcare

Paying for insurance is a way of managing risk by transferring the cost of a potential loss to the insurance company, who will usually pay out when there is a claim. This involves paying a monthly or annual premium calculated based on your circumstances and risk. Most people will have motor insurance in the UK because it is a legal requirement for drivers. We can also insure our homes, travel and other valuables. Healthcare (and dental) plans are also available - this is very important in countries where there is no free National Health Service (NHS). Insurance for income protection and critical illness cover is also becoming more popular among professionals, who will often also have professional indemnity fees to pay yearly in order to keep practising. Add this also to life insurance cover, and the money we might be spending on insurance premiums can add up to quite a chunk of our income.

Sadly, people with health problems can sometimes struggle to find suitable or affordable insurance cover. This can be because of challenges at the application stage, which someone with mental health problems might find difficult to navigate, or because of limited income due to their inability to work. Having insurance gives people peace of mind from knowing that they do not have to fork out huge sums of money if a disaster occured. The insurance company will only pay out if you have been completely truthful about pre-existing conditions, including mental health problems. The Equality Act 2010 (England and Wales) protects people from disability discrimination, but insurance companies can still lawfully refuse to cover someone or decide to charge them a higher premium when acting on relevant and reliable information, in a reasonable way. There are charities, like Mind, that can support people with mental health conditions to find insurance and check that they are being treated lawfully.

The financial strain from unexpected problems when there is no insurance cover can be very stressful, even for someone who has not been diagnosed with a mental health condition. This is especially true if people have no savings or access to credit. In countries like America where you need to present your insurance details to access health care, even the excess charge can be a shock to one's finances, at a time when they are also worried about their health. Some people who desperately need the care might get government aid or take on huge amounts of debt from healthcare bills, which they have to pay off over time. This can put a lot of pressure on families, especially where there is a child with a chronic health condition, for example. Parents might become depressed or anxious because of bills they cannot keep up with, in spite of having more than one job. The sick family member might also feel like a burden because of the financial difficulty their condition is causing for the family. They might even get thoughts of hopelessness, guilt and suicide. Even in countries where healthcare is free at the point of delivery, other associated costs might be a burden to low income families. Some might struggle to afford transportation costs for hospital appointments, parking fees and prescription charges. This becomes additional stress at a time when they are worried about the health of their loved one.

It is well known that people with chronic conditions and pain are more likely to experience depression. Adding financial and mental strain to the physical aspects of their condition can make it even more difficult to face each day. People might also make unwise health choices motivated by lack of money. This is especially true for dental care in the UK where most adults have to pay for dental appointments. People might go years without a dental check up, or persevere with dental pain/symptoms for months, for lack of money to get proper treatment in a timely manner. Even the NHS subsidised dental fees might be too much for a worker who is struggling to keep up with basic bills. Thankfully, those in full time education, children, pregnant women, new mothers and those receiving low income benefits do not have to pay for NHS dental services in England. People who are doing well financially have the option of NHS/private dental treatments and other aesthetic options to look and feel good. The ability to pay comfortably for treatments and insurance thereby having an impact on their different perspectives of the same health issues.

The impact of poverty and wealth on health can often be seen long before people present to hospitals or dentists. For example, there are significant inequalities in oral health for children living in deprived communities compared to those living in affluent communities. Poor children will usually have a less healthy diet and higher rates of obesity as well. Sadly, poor oral health affects their

ability to function and socialise, leading to more disadvantages, especially when they have to regularly miss
school because of pain, infections or hospital admissions.
Even though most people understand the benefits of
healthy eating, sugar reduction, regular dental checks and
daily teeth hygiene, it is difficult for someone living in deprivation to put this into practice especially when
struggling with childcare, financial and mental stress. It is
also sometimes easier to let the children have sweets and
fizzy drinks, ignore follow up dental appointments and
leave out night time brushing in a stressful home environment. If people are struggling with their finances and
mental health, they might find it hard to concentrate and
plan their meals or diary, leading to even more chaos and
consequences. Unfortunately, this leads to more financial
and health problems so that the cycle of poverty and stress
continues. There are time management and stress management tips shared in my earlier book, *Life Without
Coffee (Choosing Happiness Over Stress),* for people who
want to break out of such unhelpful patterns.

Binge eating can also be part of the mental health condition, bulimia. It is an eating disorder where people can eat
a lot of food, then make themselves vomit, use laxatives or
exercise excessively to avoid weight gain. It is most common among teenagers, and stomach acid from the

recurrent vomiting may damage their teeth. Anxiety, low self esteem, previous sexual abuse and having a family history of similar mental health conditions can make people more likely to develop an eating disorder. There is medical help available, which might include Cognitive Behavioural Therapy or family therapy. This is again another motivation to manage our finances and time wisely to give our children a better chance of good mental health, and reduce strain on ours. It might seem like a lot of money to pay for healthy options and medical check ups when we feel well, but we can consider it an investment in our future health and that of our family. It is surely cheaper to pay for fruits and vegetables now, than to pay for regular diabetes medication or psychotherapy in future. It might seem financially foolish to work part time in certain phases of life to spend time with our families to improve their mental health, diet, self esteem and ours, but it will surely pay off when we do not have to spend money repairing the damage done from years of neglect, stress or even abuse. Healthcare is a major cost for a lot of people in midlife and old age because of some lifestyle choices which have led to obesity, diabetes, high blood pressure, financial stress, depression/anxiety and associated complications.

This is not to say that we should live in regret or guilt. We can always learn from the past and move on with wisdom. It is still worth making time for exercise, healthy eating and communication with family/friends now to reduce our risk of physical and mental health problems in the future. There is good evidence that a healthy lifestyle can reduce your risk of dementia in old age. Age, genes and education level are risk factors that can be hard to change, but a healthy diet, healthy weight, healthy blood pressure and regular exercise can also reduce your risk. It is best to avoid smoking and alcohol excess as well. Dementia has also been associated with untreated depression, loneliness or social isolation and a sedentary lifestyle. If financial problems can increase risk of depression and social isolation, then it makes sense to also avoid financial stress to reduce risk of dementia.

Some people might need social care as they get older, especially if they have dementia or other conditions that mean that they are unable to care for themselves. This can be a significant cost to the person or their family also. The social care system, even in wealthier countries, is struggling with lack of sufficient funds. Insurance can sometimes help with these costs, but we need to have planned for it in advance with regular payments to reduce the strain when the time comes. Social care and health care are connected. We see older people who have recurrent hospital admissions because they are unable to cope at home due to poor diet, poor mobility and poor selfcare leading to infections, falls, depression and other complications of chronic conditions. The stress of looking after elderly relatives, especially when people have mental and financial problems of their own, can be quite crippling. Some patients even drop out of the workforce for years because of the strain on their mental health. It is important to manage finances wisely for this, because the emotional strain alone, even when money is not an issue, can be quite significant.

Reflection

- Are you currently spending less or more than you earn?
- What are your three biggest regular expenses?
- Does your current budget (and bank statement) reflect your values and priorities?
- What percentage of your income goes towards planning for your future (e.g savings, investments, pensions and insurance)?
- Which financial resources (e.g podcasts, books, advisers, videos, charities or websites) can you access this year to improve your knowledge and skills around managing money?

Part 4

How Money Affects Relationships

4.1 - Give and Take

This section is really about dependent relationships where one has responsibility to provide money or other needs for the other. This is most obvious in a parent-child relationship, where small children cannot earn money and depend on their parents to meet their needs. The parent feels responsible for the child and feels good to be able to live up to his/her responsibility to provide, whether the child appreciates it or not. Obviously a grateful and responsible child will bring joy to hard working parents, but a wasteful and lazy child will cause them sorrow. The relationship evolves as children grow, because we expect more from older, healthy children, after spending so much to raise them. They grow to become more independent and able to make good choices for their own lives. Eventually, they can earn their own money and not need so much financial support from their parents, if things go well.

Relationships can become complicated when parents exert a lot of control over adult children, especially if they are still financially dependent on them. In certain cultures, children are expected to pay rent and other bills once they turn 18. They might move out of the family house and get their own place, especially if they do not wish to pursue higher education. In other cultures, people are considered dependent children until they get married. Even the marriage partner and friends might have to be chosen with parental influence. A single person in their 30s might still have rent and bills paid by their parents, live with their parents and even have their parents controlling how they spend their earnings. It is not always about the parents being wealthier and controlling, it is sometimes seen as a matter of culture and respect for elders. If the parents are paying for higher education or supporting the adult financially, there can be serious conflict when the children make life choices that the parents are not happy with. Even though parents will normally care about what their children do, money makes the relationship more complicated because they can sometimes feel that they have more of a say in the person's choices. Such conflict is not always verbalised, and adult children sometimes feel unable to say what they really want or feel, for fear of being cut off financially. Somehow, the one who pays the bills often gets to have the final say, which might be detrimental to the mental health of the receiver who lacks autonomy over their own affairs.

In cultures where adult children work to support poorer parents, there might be a level of financial abuse where the adult child feels bullied into spending money in ways they would rather not, because saying no would be considered disrespectful and selfish. They slave away for years with no financial progress because their finances are being managed poorly by parents who do not know any better. Circles of poverty continue until someone is brave enough to break out of the web, or try another way of managing money, if the parents are open-minded. Sometimes, the supported parents might be the ones experiencing depression and low self esteem because the young breadwinner, who has all the money, makes all the decisions without taking their desires into consideration. Their adult child might be stressed from supporting siblings as well, as is the case in some African cultures, and just makes decisions for the family without considering what people really want. Some families might be grateful for the financial support, but others might feel entitled and ungrateful. Relatives might even get bitter or jealous of a successful person who is working hard to give them what he/she can. When people feel bitter or entitled, they might even lie to or steal from the working relative due to greed or need for some autonomy. Most of us value the opportunity to make our own decisions and lead a life of our choosing. Money can give us options, and whoever controls the money usually controls the options available to us. Instead of feeling envious, depressed or resentful of the one who makes and controls the money, it is better to focus our energy on improving ourselves and becoming independent too.

Employers are responsible for paying their employees for work done, as agreed in their employment contract. This makes the employer the boss, and the worker must earn that wage. Even though there are laws to protect the rights of employees, many people feel like slaves in their jobs because they need the money and would not be there otherwise. They might feel angry or envious of employers and managers, if they do not feel that they are being treated fairly or respectfully. Some bosses let the power get to their heads, and speak to workers in unacceptable ways, just because they feel they can get away with it. The silence of a respectful worker must never be taken for weakness, because they will get their own back whenever they get the chance. It is always better to maintain an atmosphere of mutual respect in workplaces, so that people can give their best and have the best interest of the company at heart. Evidence shows that happy workers are more productive, with less absenteeism. In the studies, happier workers used the time they had more effectively and increased their pace without sacrificing quality. One company saw a rise of up to 37% in employee satisfaction when they invested in employee support.

The dynamics between employees can also be affected by money, especially if they are competing for promotions, recognition and bonuses. Some people express their insecurities and poor mental health by bullying other workers or being overly critical of their work. Unhappy workers can cost companies thousands of pounds through less productivity and more sick leave. We often see people asking for weeks off work with stress because of conflict at work, bullying and burnout. Investing in team building is a great place to start, considering the fact that many people spend most of their waking hours at work. Having a positive and happy work environment is good for the mental health and productivity of staff, when they are pleased to be at work. Team building encourages staff to socialise, collaborate and work together healthily to achieve the greater goals of the organisation, instead of competing and pulling each other down in ways that cause stress, anxiety, depression and insomnia. Good teams with good social relationships are beneficial for the mental health of employees.

Another give and take relationship is that of organisations and clients, where the company depends on payments and reviews from clients to be successful. According to the popular saying - the customer is always right. We do all in our power to ensure their satisfaction, but how do we deal with difficult clients? Most organisations will have a complaints procedure to help unhappy customers, but how is the relationship affected when a paying client is actually in the wrong? There must be procedures in place to protect the rights of workers, in spite of the company's desire for more money or client satisfaction. Health care organisations usually have a zero tolerance policy for staff abuse, for example, which helps to look after the mental health of staff doing such stressful, public-facing roles. In some other institutions, managers turn a blind eye to (sexual) harrassment or discrimination towards staff as long as the company gets to keep a big client or valuable consultant. The staff member, who needs the job, might not feel empowered to quit, complain or sue. This then has a negative effect on their self esteem and mental health, as they carry on experiencing more humiliation at work for the sake of money. Even though the person paying the bills usually has the final say, it is important to have boundaries/standards and do what we can to maintain our self respect. There are charities and government organisations that can support people in such situations to raise grievances and get compensation, if they have to leave such jobs.

Complex family dynamics can be made worse when money is involved and not handled wisely. With the rise in numbers of "blended families" because of couples getting together after a divorce/separation, there will be parents sending financial support for children they do not normally live with, who may feel entitled to more time or money than they are getting. This can also affect the finances in the parent's new home, where they might now have children with the new partner, who may not be too pleased about being financially affected in this way. Paying child maintenance does not count as shared finances, but such regular expenses might have an impact on your shared mortgage or other borrowing, which can affect your credit rating. Being married to someone or sharing the same address with them does not make you financial associates for the purpose of credit scoring, but having a joint bank account, joint mortgage, joint loan or a joint county court judgement will. Having a low credit score can negatively affect a financial associate's ability to get credit, even if you are not applying together, so it is important to think carefully before making financial associations, especially when there are additional factors to be considered. Relationships can become more difficult when people feel that someone (such as a step child, step parent or ex-wife) is to blame for their inability to get the things they want, such as a bigger mortgage/house/allowance, because of additional financial commitments. Such resentment can be displayed through words and attitudes that can be unhelpful to all involved. In some cases, there is plenty of money to go around and the parent lives up to his/her responsibilities, but people might still struggle with negative thinking and stress that is not beneficial for their mental health. It is better to live in peace as much as possible, and realise that more is not always better.

Some parents, especially where father and mother are no longer together, might feel guilty for putting their children through a divorce, and overcompensate with money and gifts. This is something some parents do, even without this excuse, because they feel that giving children whatever they want is a sign of love. The problem with this pattern of giving is that it makes children believe that they can have whatever they want in life, so they are unable to cope with disappointment and periods of scarcity in adulthood. No matter how rich you are, there will eventually be something your child wants in future that you will have no control over, and cannot give it to them. If you are unfortunate to have a change in financial circumstances also, and become unable to grant their every desire as they have become so accustomed to, without understanding how lucky they were, you could all struggle to cope mentally. Some people have driven themselves into crime/fraud/debt to keep up with the expectations of their spoiled children, causing themselves untold mental stress and eventually harming the future of the children they love so much. While it is nice to be able to provide for children, it is also the responsibility of parents to teach them the value of money, contentment and self control.

4.2 - Two become One

A third of adults with partners report that money is a big source of conflict in their relationships. This is not just about having too little money - even people with a lot of money can have relationship problems because of how money is managed. These problems are usually there before people commit to marriage, and get magnified as time goes on, especially when children come into the equation. The whole idea of marriage is that two become one, but many still lead individual lives in marriage, especially in the area of finances. Working couples might decide to split bills and avoid difficult conversations about money, so that each partner carries on spending as they wish. Although this might seem like a fair and easy way of doing things, it leads to bigger problems in future, for example if one partner loses their job, has a career change or another change in circumstances. This system also robs couples of the benefits of working together financially to achieve more, such as saving to buy a house, making other investments or preparing for retirement. Couples need to have open discussions about debt and financial goals in advance, so that they can tackle them together and make plans for rainy days. These discussions can be difficult because people have different personalities, even in the ways that they handle money. Our past experiences and goals for the future can affect the way we spend and save. These money habits can also change in different seasons of life, so regular honest communication is key to having good relationships, which is important for mental wellbeing.

According to 2019 Office of National Statistics (ONS) data, "unreasonable behaviour" was the most common reason cited for divorce in England and Wales. A survey showed that money worries were one of the main reasons for breaking up, leading to an increase in divorce rates over the past six decades. Sadly, the cost of divorce itself can be significant, especially because of legal costs, leaving people in a more difficult financial situation afterwards. The Married Couple's Allowance in the UK can give couples a little reduction in tax bills to ease financial pressure, but government schemes like this have not been enough to save marriages where there are serious relationship problems. Working together through money issues can be complicated where there is a power play, such as one partner earning more or coming from a richer family, difficulty finding work when both partners wish to work, or in cases where one partner chooses not to work. It might be difficult to admit the emotional and mental health effects of these scenarios, but that does not mean that they do not exist. Transparency and joint accounts for equal access to money might help to manage such dynamics, but cannot replace the importance of communication and cooperation. When people live in a situation that constantly makes them feel inferior or inadequate, they can develop low self esteem, depression or even anxiety. Little actions like giving the lower earner charge over some spending decisions can help to improve their sense of control and mental health. Although, it is always better for the couple to let the person who is better at managing money (whether man or woman) handle the majority of expenses and accounting.

Managing finances in marriage becomes even trickier when children and extended family are considered. It is worth discussing expectations regarding having children and how related costs and sacrifices will be managed, before it happens. While we cannot plan for every possible scenario, we can try to make sure that we are on the same page as couples in terms of our vision and goals. Some people decide to take career breaks while children are very young, or may want to have big families with many children. The financial implication of these choices should be discussed, so that couples can work together to find a solution that both are happy with. Some couples engage the help of grandparents for childcare to save costs, but that might also open doors to other extended family issues that were not accounted for. Couples might have to work together to support their parents in financial difficulty, but if there is no agreement on how this is done, it can lead to serious conflict because of the significant effect on the couple's finances. Sometimes, money can cause relationship strain when grandparents or other relatives buy expensive gifts for the couple or their children that in-laws cannot afford to match, or partners struggle to accept. It is important to be united and set boundaries as a couple when dealing with extended family.

The anxiety that some people feel around protecting their personal money and assets in marriage, has led to a rise in prenuptial and even postnuptial marital contracts. It may feel insulting or look unreasonable to others, but if this is something that might give you peace of mind, there are family lawyers that can support couples with this option. There are legal costs to be considered though, because each partner must get legal advice by a separate lawyer for such agreements to be valid. Even without a legal contract, it is important to be open to each other about assets and debt in marriage, because most of the anxiety people feel comes from a fear of the unknown - secrets we worry might come out to destroy us. You would hate to be working all hours and giving your all in marriage, only to find out that your partner is servicing debts, making commitments or hiding assets you knew nothing about. Lack of trust and financial fidelity breaks up marriages long before the divorce is official.

Thankfully, many marriages are getting along well, in spite of occasional conflicts about money. People learn to understand each other better and find ways to work together in spite of their differences. It is important to grow together also, because people change with time. What was very important to one partner ten years ago might not be a priority now. Regular and sensitive communication is key. Couples can regularly discuss their desires and ideas as their circumstances change, so that they are able to make the most of every situation and feel good about making progress as a family. It can be depressing to watch other couples making progress, while you stay stagnant in life due to poor financial planning in marriage. There will be seasons where one or both partners have to work long hours to achieve some goals that will be good for the family eventually, but those tough seasons can be made easier emotionally if the couple is in agreement and each partner feels supported. It is always better to discuss the impact of such sacrifice and agree as a family before making any commitments, to avoid resentment. We see people losing their marriages because they thought that working long hours or taking frequent business trips to make more money would make their spouse happy, but it actually left them feeling neglected and unloved. Money truly does not buy happiness, and we do not want to lose priceless things in the pursuit of more money. On the other hand, some people sacrifice their careers to stay home (e.g. with children or elderly relatives) on the assumption that their partner does not mind being the sole earner. They look back later on their sacrifice with regret when one partner leaves the marriage because they felt unsupported, overworked and unattracted to their spouse.

There are several factors that contribute to our choice of work, wants and financial goals. Where we live/work, the type of schools children attend, cars we drive, clothes we wear, things we do for fun can all affect our bills, regular spending and mental health. As married couples, it is important to understand the "why?" for each other. Some people will gladly invest every penny they have to pursue a business idea or dream, looking foolish to everyone else, except the spouse that understands them. It might not even make complete sense to the spouse, but they choose to be supportive and understanding. Having someone else on our team financially can help us to see past our emotional drive and make more sensible financial decisions that are not just driven by passion or a desire to "keep up with the Jones'. It is a shame to lose this benefit of marriage if people continue to act independently of each other when it comes to finances. When couples agree, they can work together to make a bigger success and less stress of the ideas they choose to run with. Couples can seek help from financial advisers or counsellors to discuss tricky money issues and help them to make more sound financial decisions that are not just being made to keep one partner happy, or look good (even in debt). They will both be happy when investments pay off and there is less financial stress in future because of better choices now.

4.3 - Love in Cash

In Nigeria, the term Mugu/Maga is used to describe someone who is easily fooled for money. It is not just scammers that use this term, ordinary people can take advantage of their friends and family's love and generous nature to get money from them that they did not really need. We hear of people working two jobs with no rest, while their unemployed relatives in Africa enjoy comfortable lifestyles at their expense. The money relationship in such families is what I describe as "love in cash". When people do not just call to check up on each other or share life experiences, when every phone call or conversation translates to money requests or when you are expected to cough up money whenever you show concern, that is not a healthy relationship. People can no longer just say "Congratulations" when someone has a baby or gets married, they are expected to "send something" as well. If someone with a job/income (a worker) asks for an update about a family problem, they are expected to send money to solve it, as a show of their love and concern. Sometimes, these expectations are mostly in the head of the worker, because people will only behave in the way we allow them to towards us. It is funny also that when the worker/sender has a baby or gets married, those same people never send them "something". It is usually a one-way money relationship. They even ask for more money when they hear that the sender has just bought a car or house, forgetting that they have just had a huge expense. They make you feel too guilty or scared to share your success stories. They believe you must be very wealthy to have made such a purchase and try to take whatever they can get from you still, in what is called "awoof". This is usually nothing to do with how rich or poor the people are, but how greedy, wicked or irresponsible they really are. I have seen people with next to nothing bring small local gifts for a relative visiting from afar, while those with good jobs and houses visit them just to see what they can get. Most workers are not fools. When they reflect and realise that giving has been a one-way street and certain people only care about what they can get, it is depressing for the generous relative. The givers can also become very anxious, suspicious or emotionally detached, especially where they have been scammed of huge amounts by trusted loved ones in the past.

We might sometimes put undue financial pressure on ourselves as workers because of our "saviour mentality", as discussed previously, because we do not know any other way to express love or concern for friends or family. Such issues have even led to marital problems and relationship breakdown when one's partner is not willing to make foolish financial decisions or go into debt to keep up with such pressure. This is something I would describe as a background factor affecting mental health, but also causing financial stress that can lead to more health problems. I will never forget a middle-aged African patient I saw who had very high blood pressure and was advised to go to hospital for treatment. She refused to go, but came to my doctor's office/surgery the next day. When asked why she did not get urgent treatment as advised, she explained how she was working all the time to support her adult relatives abroad, with no time to rest. When I explained the risk of stroke with such high blood pressure, she told me that she secretly hoped the condition would kill her so she could get out of these commitments! People from certain cultures would rarely ever admit suicidal thoughts or discuss mental health issues, but this is clearly a case of depression and hopelessness, which her family may be unaware of because she puts on a brave face and keeps sending money as a show of love/care. It is sometimes also a matter of pride and duty, or appearing successful. For her, it was unthinkable to draw boundaries and tell them she could no longer afford to keep giving them money regularly. She was probably also not able to save or plan for her retirement because of these issues, and saw no end to her suffering. Even when some people try to talk to their relatives about the financial stress they are facing with too many demands, they get told to stop complaining, have faith, be more positive and give cheerfully so they can be "blessed". This is usually from adults who should be working and earning their own money, or coping with the little they have, but are selfishly taking money from a relative who has their own family to support. It is a good thing for families to be able to help each other out in tough times, and that is what love is about. Sharing and community is good for our mental health. The problem starts when people cannot really afford to help but feel compelled to, when people take advantage of the worker's kindness and do not work hard or plan ahead to handle their own responsibilities, and when it becomes an ongoing stressful issue that becomes detrimental to the giver's mental health. Those receiving money regularly enjoy the benefits of passive income at the expense of their relative or friend's sweat, tears, physical and mental health. Surely, that is not love.

Love in cash is when you cannot visit relatives or friends just to spend time together, but feel the need to bring something as a sign of love/care, whether you can afford it or not, because hugs and kisses are not good enough. When time together or phone calls are no longer of value, because money or gifts are preferred. When you would rather not pay for a flight or train home because you do not have enough to buy gifts for everyone you will meet there. When your friends are only friends in good times, and disappear as soon as you have no money to pay for the drinks or parties. When a romantic relationship ends when one loses his/her source of income, or when the expensive gifts stop flowing. People enjoy receiving cash/gifts as expressions of love, but do not realise the mental health implications and power dynamics of such one-way relationships. Some people get treated like prostitutes and property in a relationship, because there is no true love. Money helps to solve a lot of problems, gets us places and can help us buy so many things, but should not be allowed to replace love in any relationship, especially not among family members. This is the kind of mentality that makes it possible for someone richer to "steal" a friend or destroy a family's unity. Some people have developed this mentality because of years of poverty, but it can be unlearned once identified. Part of our work at Forte Charity for Inspiration is to help people change their mindset about money, promote integrity, help young people gain an education and stand on their own two feet financially, so they do not need to be in such unhealthy and parasitic relationships, which can be stressful and detrimental to mental health in the long run.

4.4 - Cash is King

I used to hate this phrase, until I finally understood its meaning. It simply refers to the fact that cash gives individuals, businesses and investors an advantage in tough times and financial flexibility to take advantage of opportunities that come up. Money experts advise people to have three to six months (living) expenses saved as emergency funds, in case they lose their source of income. It might need to be more or less depending on your lifestyle and industry. Having easily accessible cash can be of benefit in times of financial uncertainty, so people do not have to sell off shares and assets, for example, at low prices in desperation. Keeping some liquid cash (not necessarily notes and coins) might not be the most profitable investment decision, but might be helpful for your mental health, especially if you have an anxious personality. Building up large amounts of cash and keeping it safe from wasteful spending takes a lot of discipline. This is the reason why some people prefer to keep cash to a minimum and keep their money tied up in investments. It is important to know yourself and what will work best for your future and mental health. There is always the option of medium term investments or having a separate bank for such savings, whilst being aware of the impact of inflation.

In a society that mostly runs on credit, it is a breath of fresh air to see some people spending their own cash - not loans, credit cards or overdrafts. You feel more in control when you do not need to wait for bank approval for a loan or mortgage before you go ahead with your purchase or project. People able to pay cash can often get better deals for certain purchases and services. You may have noticed that even insurance premiums are cheaper when you pay annually, instead of monthly. There is a big difference between the relationship a bank has with regular customers (i.e borrowers) and people with lots of cash. It is still important to understand how the financial system works where you live, so that you can maintain a good credit rating, in case you ever need to prove your creditworthiness, but it is best not to get fooled into becoming a slave of the credit system. Cash really does affect relationships and options. Some people are literally working to make several repayments, because it can be so easy to get houses, cars and other things with little or no cash deposit. The number of "Buy now, pay later" schemes are on the increase - even for the smallest things. We often forget that banks are out to make money, and interest rates matter. Half of adults with debt have a mental health problem, because getting into debt can cause and be caused by mental health problems. It might seem easier to ignore financial problems that make us feel guilty, hopeless or anxious, but sorting out money issues can help people feel better. When we are in sound mind, we can compare interest rates (if borrowing is necessary) and go for the best options instead of buying things or taking loans because of speed, impulse and convenience. Exciting purchases on credit and fast loans can make people feel happy momentarily, but the burden of huge/several re-payments over years can be detrimental to mental health and relationships. Some people have even ended up in bankruptcy, divorce or psychiatric hospitals.

Nothing good comes easy. If you also agree that "cash is king" and see the advantages, you can make a long term plan now to get out of the repayments lifestyle by cutting down your expenses, paying off debts and building your savings. This is not about getting greedy for money or do-ing anything to have cash and be king. Remember that the love of money is the root of all evil. Slow and steady wins the race, as they say. Most millionaires did not start with six-figure salaries. It is all about managing what we have wisely and being humble enough to acknowledge what we cannot afford. When people work hard and man-age their money well to have cash advantage, they can choose to use it for good or bad purposes. We hear of peo-ple using their money to entice and groom vulnerable adults/children for their own gain/pleasure. The abuser usually has the upper hand in the relationship because of the money and gifts they can provide for the victim. When we realise that money is not everything, we can choose to say no and go without for a while, in order to protect our dignity and mental health. Unfortunately, the victim in most cases is someone of poor mental health. Some people use their money for bribery and corruption - bending rules for selfish gain. They feel above the law because of the money they have and the people around them that worship money or material things. There is a lot of dead conscience in such scenarios, which leads to even more illegal activities until they lose their peace of mind and wonder why they suffer ill health.

The benefits of having cash can be used for good purposes when people are able to give more, without worrying about their bank balance. Having plenty of money is a big responsibility that not many people can handle. Even if we do not need a lot of money for ourselves, we can look around at those in poverty to find the motivation to take advantage of the financial opportunities we have, so that we can have more to give to charity. There are so many people who might never earn more than a certain amount because of limitations in their circumstances and mentality. Being able to earn more than we can spend is a privilege. There are so many charitable projects and organisations that can benefit from our giving, and the advantage that cash brings. Some people are able to give their children (or parents) large amounts of money to buy houses, or pay for life events like their weddings or anniversary celebrations. Having money to do good things can also open doors that no amount of speech will. People might feel closer to and tend to listen more to the person that was able to help them in tough times, because cash was what they really needed. It is important to be aware of this money effect in relationships though, because money and gifts do not equal love, even though they can sometimes bring favour. Politicians in corrupt systems often use money to win the hearts of local leaders and elections. When we are aware of the effect of money on such relationships, we can be more intentional about managing conflicts of interest and living with integrity for the sake of our mental health and reputation.

4.5 - No Friends in Business

Most of us have heard of relationships that went sour once money got involved. Even the best of friends can become enemies when they have to share money or when they become business partners. This is the reason why people are advised not to lend money (in amounts they cannot give away) to family or friends. Circumstances might change, causing the person to break the repayment agreement, which can lead to resentment, stress and relationship break down. Not many relationships can survive the strain of money problems, but we can overcome anything when we value people and relationships over money. Refusal or inability to repay a loan given in good faith can be very hurtful, especially when we believe that someone has taken us for granted and not kept their word, putting us in a difficult situation we did not expect. It can lead to dark and negative thoughts that are unhelpful for our mental health. Sometimes, this happens when we feel cheated out of our fair share of profit and reward from doing business together. One may have started a business relationship with a friend, believing that there will be 50/50 contribution in effort and share of profits, but later realise that the friend is lazier or less competent than they thought. The constant stress from making up for their inadequacies can put a strain on your mental and physical strength. Loved ones might even get annoyed for you, especially when the person insists on taking full payment after doing less work. There can be difficult conversations to be had, which some people tend to avoid because of their personalities. Bottling up issues to avoid confrontation can lead to more depression, anger and financial stress, which can later affect earning power and work prospects.

Some relationships start from work and end up becoming personal friendships. Where money is involved, it is important to have boundaries and draw up written contracts to avoid confusion. People can say things they do not mean or make promises they cannot keep when they are happy or upset. Having written agreements is helpful to reduce stress and misunderstanding. The workplace can become unbearable when there is tension because of financial disagreements. People might have made life plans and budgets based on money they expected to get, so it can have a serious financial impact when promises are broken or when people feel cheated or betrayed. The dynamics of friendship can also be affected when a friend becomes an employer, employee, client or business partner. It is important to communicate expectations clearly, especially around money, to avoid problems. People sometimes run into problems because we expect "mates rates" or feel awkward to charge friends/family members, even to the detriment of our business. We need to be clear about whether we are running a business or a charity. There is nothing wrong with offering discounts or bonuses to family or friends, but charges/fees/dividends/salaries need to be clearly explained before commitment is made on either side, to avoid confusion and disagreement. A friend might be willing to support your business, but may not have the means to pay the rates you expect. They may also have the means, but not the understanding that they still need to pay for services, even if their friend/relative owns the business. Others might assume that you do not mind working for free or paying them more, because of previous favours you or they have done. It is always better to have the awkward conversation sooner, rather than later; or if you really cannot manage it, try to keep business/work and friendships/family apart.

There are successful family businesses everywhere, but some are ridden with tales of betrayal, greed, bitterness and envy where the love of money has become stronger than the value people place on relationships. The story of the Gucci family from Italy is a very sad example. Family businesses can provide work for family members, status in the community and long term financial security. Given the prevalence of mental illness and its association with social and occupational activities, it is understandable that some people working in family businesses will also experience mental health problems. Some family businesses were actually set up to provide employment for family members with mental health problems, such as anxiety, depression and Attention Deficit Hypersensitivity Disorder (ADHD), who might struggle to get employment elsewhere. People with ADHD can be restless, impulsive and have poor concentration, which other employers might not tolerate. As conditions like ADHD tend to run in families, relatives might be more understanding of the condition and able to accommodate each other to use their strengths and create a source of income, outside of traditional work settings. All families experience stressful events, which can have an impact on relationships and family business. Research suggests that coping strategies and family resources have a greater impact on how a family adapts to someone with mental illness, than the severity of the mental illness itself. Because family and work roles can often overlap when relatives work together, it might be advantageous for the mental health of those struggling, but can also lead to work conflict and reduced performance. There might be complications that affect financial wellbeing of the business when an incompetent leader cannot be dethroned, or employees feel entitled or demotivated. There can also be overprotection of incompetent family members, reduction in talent pool (when others cannot thrive in that environment), negative emotional atmosphere and regular need to manage family tension, which is not good for the mental health of all involved.

If making money is the main purpose of business or work relationships, we need to be aware of how mental health can affect this, so that we can put emotions (friends/family) aside and make better financial decisions. We can also choose to be intentional, for the sake of peace and a fuller life, to accept less profit/income, in order to maintain the relationships we value, in spite of possible tension and reduced profit. It is very important to be aware of how much power and access to funds people have, especially when they are struggling with their mental health. A depressed and pessimistic boss might decide to sell the business because of his bleak view of the future, someone with mania or narcissistic personality disorder may spend company funds recklessly, and someone with anxiety may bypass good business opportunities for fear of losses. Getting into a business partnership has been described to be as serious as marriage in some cases. We need to choose carefully who we associate with. It can be difficult to see some aspects of people's personality before getting into business with them, so it is wise to have a good exit plan for if things do not go well.

There is a popular saying - "Show me your friends, and I will tell you who you are". It is sometimes adjusted to say, "Show me your friends, and I will show you your future". This is also relevant for money habits. When we regularly associate with people who overspend, are materialistic, lazy, hard working, envious, content, greedy or stingy, their attitudes can rub off on us. If we spend most of our waking hours at work, we need to be intentional about who we spend time with at work. There might be situations where we have to work with people we do not like or admire, but we can control how much influence we let them have on us personally when we recognise characteristics we do not like. You can usually tell what people are like by their attitude to money and how they treat people they do not have to be nice to. People who are materialistic, spend their time comparing themselves to others and always wanting what other people have, can make us start to feel unhappy and dissatisfied with life. People who have a poverty mindset and enjoy begging or borrowing will either become financial parasites to you or draw you into that mindset. It is better to surround ourselves with friends who challenge us to do well. Sadly, family members and coworkers are not always our best friends, but friends are the family we choose for ourselves.

Reflection

- Do you currently have anyone that depends on you regularly for money/provision?
- What would your relationships look like, if money was not involved?
- Do you have any relationships that have become difficult because of money or debt?
- Are there ways that you might be allowing yourself to be used or that you might be taking advantage of others financially?
- Are there any changes you could make today to restore peace, respect and fairness in your relationships?

Part 5
How to Look After Our Mental Health

5.1 – Priorities

It is easier to prioritise when we have a clear vision for our lives. Where do you see yourself in 10, 20, 40 or 60 years? Some goals are short term, others are long term, but they all need to fit in with the vision we have for our lives. We can then manage money and time with respect to those goals that fit in with our vision and priorities. Having goals and achieving them is good for our mental health and self esteem. Even knock-backs can be handled better when we have a bigger perspective. Some people use the start of each new year to set goals and review their priorities, but this can be done at any time of the year, to decide what the priorities are for this stage/phase of your life. If you have a family or special relationships in your life, it is important to review how the use of your time and money reflects the value you place on these. It is difficult to believe that family is your number one priority when your diary and bank statement show otherwise. Many of us work hard and want to do our best for our loved ones and future, but it should not be to the detriment of our close relationships, spirituality and mental health. It is all about finding a good balance. Jesus Christ famously asked, "For what shall it profit a man, if he shall gain the whole world, but lose his soul?"

Because time and money are finite, we will have to learn to say "no" to some things, in order for us to be able to say "yes" (later) to the things that matter most to us. We cannot keep saying "yes" to spending £100 unnecessarily here and there, expecting to still be able to save £10,000 for the project or house we dream of. Some of the things we say "no" to might even be good things like giving to charities, extended family, nice holidays and work opportunities that might be too demanding on our time, but it will all make sense when we have clear priorities and vision for our lives. People who are sensible and actually care about us will usually understand. Make time regularly for rest and relax with loved ones, no matter how busy your work is. It does not have to be expensive holidays or weeks off work, it can just be a few quality hours that leave you feeling refreshed and ready to face the world again. Making time for family and friends will give them much more than money can buy. They feel loved, valued and appreciated. If all else fails at work or business, they will be the ones that will be there for you. I heard somewhere that no one ever said on their deathbed that they wished they spent more time at work!

Keep an eye on the big picture, even when focusing on the small projects. Be intentional with what you allow to bother you or change your plans. Be ready to set boundaries and know what is *not* your responsibility to handle. Your first financial responsibility is to yourself and your young children, if you have any. This is why we have family planning and contraception, so people can decide whether or not to have children. Sometimes, things can happen outside our plans, but we can reassess priorities then and still take responsibility for our own children, even if it means working harder or making some sacrifices. If you have to make sacrifices or endure tough times for a greater purpose, decide if it is worth it and how long it is likely to last, so that you can get motivation to keep going. Even if you find yourself in a job you hate, just to pay bills at the moment, you can look after your mental health by doing something you enjoy everyday, such as cooking, dancing, listening to music, working on an enjoyable side business/project or phoning a friend. Be proactive about pursuing your dream life, even if it means making daily applications for better jobs. Nothing good comes easy, but it is important to stay positive and hopeful.

If you are blessed to be doing a job you love and living a life you enjoy, it is still important to regularly review your lifestyle to ensure that it all fits with your vision and priorities. People can easily get carried away with comfort that they forget the important principles they meant to build their lives and families on. Some might get too comfortable to pray or too busy to spend time with their children, because they have no pressing needs and can now afford nannies. The Covid-19 lockdown in 2020 forced us to review our busy lifestyles when we realised we were able to cope without endless activities and just enjoy simple walks. Many people redecorated to make their homes more comfortable when they realised they had neglected the home front for too long because of busy jobs. Having a tidy, peaceful home environment with healthy routines, can be helpful if we want a home atmosphere that allows growth, productivity and relaxation.

If we value the comforts we are enjoying now, it is important to prioritise savings and investments so that we do not end up struggling financially in our later years. Realising that you will not always be able to work as much as you do in your prime will help you to prioritise paying off debts and living within your means. Financial experts generally advise people to pay off the debts with the highest interest rates first. Some people find it helpful to pay off the smallest debts first, so they can have motivation to tackle larger debts when they no longer have those repayments. It might mean cutting out some luxuries for a short while and denying ourselves some wants, in order to prioritise the goal of financial freedom and less mental stress from making several repayments and needing full-time work. Having an honest conversation with a financial adviser can be the first step in the right direction, to be able to get out of financial stress and prioritise the spending that is more important to you. There is free debt and money advice available from charities and the Citizens Advice Bureau in England. Some people dream of buying nice houses or sending their children to better schools. Dreams will forever remain dreams, if we never take action in the right direction. There are several books/videos that teach practical steps to get people achieving their financial goals, regardless of how big or small their income is.

5.2 - Communication

No man is an island - we all need each other. Talking is good for our mental health. They say, a problem shared is half-solved. If you are struggling with mental health issues relating to your finances, it helps to talk to someone you trust, even if they do not have cash to give you. Talking about it can help you find solutions and reduce tension. Lack of information is sometimes the main problem for those that struggle with their finances. If you prefer to keep your affairs private, there are charities and professionals who can help confidentially. They can signpost you to organisations that can help, and even tell you about helpful government or bank schemes, such as 0% interest credit card offers and mortgage holidays. When people struggle with their mental health, they can find it difficult to make applications and access support, making it difficult for them to get grants and benefits. It is helpful to inform a trusted friend or family member, if you are struggling in this way.

If you are married or have financial associates, honest communication is important to ensure you are all on the same page. This will reduce anxiety from secrets on both sides, and help you make better financial progress. Good communication also helps to manage expectations and find better solutions to problems, such as debt and unexpected expenses. You can discuss your financial goals and make a plan to achieve them together, which will be easier than doing things alone. It can sometimes be difficult to talk about money and spending habits, especially in marriage, but making time to talk about this (when you are both relaxed), finding what the pain points are and sensitively finding solutions will be better for your mental health, marriage and finances in the long run. This will also give your family (and children) better future prospects. We have already discussed how money problems lead to divorce and even more financial struggle after the break-up due to legal fees etc. We know that children in lone parent families have higher poverty rates, even when the parent works full-time - not to mention all the emotional stress and childcare issues, which could have been avoided with good communication and better money management. It takes two to tango. It will require some (painful) personal change, openness and humility on both sides, if there is to be unity and progress in marriage, but it can be done.

It is also important to keep open communication with your bank and creditors, even if you are struggling financially. Refusing to open letters or return phone calls does not make problems go away. Instead of waiting till you miss payments, it is better to contact your bank or creditors in advance to explain your situation. UK banks and government introduced several schemes to help people affected financially in the Covid-19 pandemic, some of which have already been mentioned. If you do not communicate with organisations, it is difficult for them to help you or signpost you to someone who can. If your financial problems are due to health issues affecting your ability to work, you can speak to your employer, occupational health department or General Practitioner (family doctor). It might be helpful to plan time off work for recovery and make arrangements to postpone or cover payments due. Missed payments can affect your credit rating and cause further financial difficulty in future, so it is best not to ignore your bills and financial commitments, even when unwell. You can also reach out to charities and other advocates that help people to communicate with big organisations in such situations.

There are times in life when we will have to work extra hard for a period to achieve certain goals. It might be working to gain a further qualification or doing more hours at work for more money to pay off debt. Some people have seasons of frequent travelling or working away from home, which can sometimes be very financially rewarding but difficult for their families. If you choose to take up such commitments or make such sacrifices to earn more and improve your prospects, it is important to communicate clearly and regularly with your loved ones, so they do not feel neglected in that season. It is even better to discuss with a spouse *before* taking on such a commitment, so that you can support each other. Be prepared to listen and make changes if the arrangement is not working. Even if you feel that it is your choice to work harder and earn more, those decisions have an impact on the time you have available for other things/people, so it is helpful if those affected understand why you are doing that and *when* they can expect things to improve. If you are unable to help people with money like they expect, it sometimes helps to explain to them that you are in a different financial situation e.g. as a student. pensioner or investor. Sometimes we might have to appear selfish to reach our financial goals and protect our mental health, before we can be able to truly help those we love, otherwise we all end up in poverty and depression. There might be a need to reduce communication with certain people who still refuse to understand and keep adding to your stress.

Communication in the workplace is important to ensure that employers and employees have reasonable expectations and job satisfaction. There will be constant emotional tension if bosses expect so much from staff but do not communicate it clearly and keep feeling disappointed. Staff can also feel unsupported, used and depressed when they expect certain things and explanations from management that they are not getting. As an employee, you need to be able to communicate any concern or problem to managers/colleagues sensibly before it becomes a bigger issue - they are not mind readers. Managers are more likely to listen when they can see that you are hardworking and have the interest of the organisation at heart. Be careful not to let your personal issues overcloud your perspective of work and undermine the effort others are making there. Some people hate their jobs because it does not suit them, not because it is not a good job. As a business owner or manager, you can set the tone of your organisation by maintaining regular communication with people in the business to make them feel valued and part of your vision. Communication is not just about telling them what to do, but also listening to their ideas and concerns to make improvements and adjust your targets, as needed. As they say, people do not leave bad jobs, they leave bad managers. When dealing with clients, good communication helps to prevent complaints and maintain a good reputation for your organisation. This will also boost staff morale and be helpful for your mental health. If you are doing business with friends/family, be clear about expectations for goods/services and payments, before proceeding. This might be awkward if you are not used to this, but will be better than having a misunderstanding or fall-out afterwards. Some people find it easier to communicate in writing or through an assistant when talking with close friends or family about money.

The most important communication is what you say to yourself. It is helpful for our mental health when we are hopeful and make positive affirmations. Be true to yourself, but remember that there is always room for improvement. Know your worth and do not feel guilty for asking for it, whether in business or employment. Get comfortable accepting credit for your hard work and do not let anyone make you feel unworthy for any reason. Be clear about your work boundaries and role, so you know when your work is done and you can rest without guilt. There is a time and season for everything. Even the 'successes' we see today have had their own share of hard times and challenges. The difference between those that give up and those that succeed is their perspective and attitude. Make time to reflect regularly and ensure you are on the right path for success. Be humble enough to take advice and learn from others, when you need to. Make self-improvement a priority by reading and learning continuously. Rome was not built in a day, and anything worth having takes time to build. We might have to learn or unlearn some habits, but when we realise the impact of financial/work stress on our mental health, we will be motivated to make the changes needed. If you are struggling with mental health issues and negative thoughts, there is free psychological help available in the UK through services such as IAPT (Improving Access to Psychological Therapy) and charities such as Mind.

5.3 - Contentment

One of the best things we can do for our mental health is to realise what stage of life we are in, be grateful for how far we have come and be hopeful for a better future. It might not be a great season right now, but we can choose to believe that it will not always be like this. Bad times will end. Even good times can come to an end. Nigerians like to say that no condition is permanent, so we can be glad that bad times can get better, and save for a rainy day in good times. There is no need to get desperate or envious of others in a different season of life. The success iceberg illustrates how success is sometimes an illusion - we do not see all the sacrifice, hard work, tears and failure that come with it. We just need to be patient and keep pressing on for our goals. It is important to have a budget that suits your current situation, instead of trying to buy or do what everyone else is doing. If you cannot afford holidays abroad, you can achieve the same rest and relaxation with a staycation. If you cannot afford expensive makeup, you can still look beautiful with cheaper or no make up. If you cannot afford expensive clothes, you can find cheaper places to shop and achieve the same looks. After all, they say a smile is the best accessory - and that costs nothing. If you cannot afford to send your children to the best schools, you can do your best with the options you have and supplement their education in other ways. Education is not just about going to school. It is far better to send children to public schools (and still have enough money/time to give them other experiences and opportunities, such as music lessons, sports clubs, travel and a healthy diet) than to struggle for years to pay expensive private school fees, having no time to spend with the family because you have to work all the time and are too stressed by money problems to teach them your own values. Private schools are great if you can afford them, but we see patients who cannot even take time off work to have surgery they need because they need to work all hours to be able to keep up with fees. If you cannot afford to get the nice new house or car you prefer, you can choose to be happy with what you have until you can afford better. Happiness is a choice. There is no guarantee that you will be happy with better stuff or in a different situation, if you have not learned to be happy and content with what you have or where you are now. There will always be more that you can want. Even people living in mansions can be unhappy because they want smaller houses or bigger mansions in nicer areas. Even people on benefits (with no job) can be unhappy because they feel their lives are also too busy or stressful. It is always a breath of fresh air to meet someone who is content with their life, and positive in spite of their challenges.

It is important to learn to budget our income and adhere to the budget as much as possible, to avoid overspending and money worries. If you regularly spend more than you earn, it is difficult to be happy with your life and income. Every month becomes a struggle because you are always broke for the last half. Instead of doing the same thing and expecting a different result, it might be time to get a pen/paper or computer, and write down your income vs expenditure. Cut out the things/bills you do not really need and try to put some money aside regularly as savings. If the main issue causing financial stress is debt/repayments, you might need to make a drastic lifestyle change to get on top of those, so you can start to enjoy your money. Most people enjoying financial freedom now have had to live on little in the past to be able to enjoy the wealth we now see. Some have been lucky enough to have parents/grandparents that did that for them, and taught them these values so they never experienced debt and poverty themselves. Wouldn't it be nice to be the one to break the debt and poverty cycle for your own family? It is so tempting to plod along with minimum payments as usual, like many people, but if we want to live free, we need to make changes others have not made, and be content in the process. Comparing yourself to others is not a good idea, especially when you are working towards financial goals. There will always be someone splashing money on parties, gifts or holidays, when you are trying to stick to a small budget. Social media does not make it easy, but we have to realise that everyone has their own struggles and budget. They might have sorted their own finances and are enjoying the results now, or will probably have to face the consequences of careless spending later.

Being content does not mean that we do not have dreams or strive for better. It is a state of happiness and satisfaction, which we can choose to enjoy wherever we live. Every decision will have its pros and cons, so contentment is not about having the best of everything. You can accept that you have no repayments for a used car, allowing you to save money for investments, projects or any car issues that might come up, without feeling bad when you meet friends with brand new cars. You can also choose to accept that a brand new or luxury car can come with monthly repayments and greater depreciation, but gives you less worry about breakdowns and a nicer image. New and old houses, private and public schools, new and used toys, designer and supermarket clothes, local and foreign holidays, employment and business, public transport or private cars/jets, luxury and average goods will all have their pros and cons, but it is important to make informed decisions that suit your budget and personality, and choose to be happy with your current life, while working towards a better future. A better future is not always about working hard, but working smart. When we manage our time and income wisely, we can create passive income streams that help us to eventually afford the nice things we want, without financial or mental stress. It is surprising to see that many "rich" people are also in financial stress. The sad thing is when we get into a financial muddle that leaves us no free cash to save or invest because we are trying so hard to keep up with the Jones', ignoring our future and putting ourselves in chronic mental stress. Some people just make decisions because that is what everyone else is doing, without knowing if they can really afford it. There are people leaving work to become stay-at-home parents or sending babies to paid childminders/nursery/daycare, because that is what their friends do - without really checking if that is the best financial decision for their family. If you have had to make a certain unpopular choice because you cannot afford other options, you might actually inspire others to think differently about their own decisions when you are content and grateful for what you have. It is amazing to see so many people getting into expensive phone contracts, TV subscriptions, gym memberships etc that add up to significant monthly outgoings, and would never consider giving them up because that is what all their friends have.

Contentment is all about perspective. Some people are having a retirement that is not as good as they planned because of unfortunate events out of their control, but they choose to accept their new reality and live content lives, instead of being bitter and envious. You can choose to be content with your job and lifestyle, while improving yourself for better opportunities in future. There is no point in envying the boss and doing a shabby job where you are, because you will end up losing even the job you despise. The one who is content and diligent in their current position could rise to be boss or entrepreneur another day. Be intentional with your time, thoughts and attitude. The things we think about soon become our words and reality. There is no shame in having little, unless it is because of laziness. When we are doing our best and find ourselves in the midst of others with more, we can choose to be inspired rather than jealous. The way we feel about ourselves can affect the way we dress and act towards others. When we are content and happy, we can be well presented, pleasant and friendly, opening doors for more opportunities and progress. I would rather work with a pleasant, confident person in clean, matching charity shop clothes, than work with someone who is unhappy, stressed and arrogant in an expensive designer suit. We do see some very rude people in cheap clothes as well. It is better to be able to wear nice clothes with a content smile and pleasant attitude when we are not financially or mentally stressed.

Work titles should not define us. You are more than your job. You are more than your looks and income. There is so much hierarchy in certain organisations and workplaces that is not helpful for mental health. It is important to have discipline and order to get work done and manage levels of responsibility, but there is no need to make people feel less valued because their job titles are not as 'important' as others. Whether you find yourself at the top or bottom of the ladder, it is wise to be kind and thoughtful towards colleagues in the workplace. Everyone has their own struggles, and we do not want to be the cause of someone else's depression or suicide. People are sometimes grumpy and rude because of their own personal problems and dissatisfaction with life, which they sadly take out on others. We can try not to take things personally when we meet such people and look after our mental health by having boundaries. If you are very unhappy in such a workplace, remember you are not a tree - move! Being kind to others and looking beyond our own personal issues to help others is also good for our own mental health. If you are blessed to have a job and mental capacity that allows you to help and care for people in your paid role, it is important to remember that what you are doing is more than a job. If you have time and energy to volunteer elsewhere or help your community in other ways, I would really encourage it. It helps to come out of our comfort zone sometimes to see less-privileged lifestyles, that will encourage us to be more grateful and content. Keeping an eye on global news is another way to stay humble and grateful, rather than feeling entitled and discontent. There are people working harder than us in other parts of the world that do not have half of what we have. Things really could be worse. Contentment and gratitude makes life more enjoyable.

5.4 - Wisdom

No one likes to think of themselves as being foolish, but the Bible says that wisdom is proved right by its results. It does not matter how long you have done something or how old you are, if the results are not good, then it might be time to wise up! There are better ways of doing things, and your way or your family's way is not always the best. Education is not just about getting qualifications, it is about opening our minds to new possibilities. There are several 'uneducated' people who manage their finances much better than professionals. You might be a very good doctor or architect, but that does not automatically mean that you know what you are doing with money and investments. It starts with the little everyday choices we make, which add up to determine how much we have to work and how much we can save/invest for the future. There are experts available to advise us, but we have to be willing to listen and sometimes even pay for their help to move forward financially. People might be hardworking and have lots of money, but little time to read and gain money wisdom available in books these days. If we choose wisdom, we can work smarter and not necessarily harder to achieve our goals. There is also wisdom in forgiving and moving on from some bad financial associations, betrayal, losses, abuse or hurt, to avoid further financial and/or mental damage.

If someone is earning a million pounds and their bills add up to just over that, they will be just as stressed as the person earning minimum wage that is just enough to cover their basic bills. Wisdom starts with knowing yourself and how you function. If there are certain things that are most important to you, which you consider a priority for your happiness, you can be intentional about budgeting for those. There will also be other regular costs that you care less about, which can be cut down. You can set limits for your spending, credit cards and phone bills, for example, so that you get a warning from your bank or service providers when you are nearing your limit, if that will help you manage your finances better. The way we teach the next generation about finances is not just through speech, but through our actions. This is especially important if you have children who watch how you spend and handle money. Do they realise the value of money and why you make certain spending decisions, or do they just think that money comes from a limitless contactless card you use in shops? Will they be able to survive life on their own as adults, if they carry on with the habits you have shown them? Some children think that eating out, taxis, hotel stays and foreign holidays are things they *must* have, not realising that these are costly things they can do without, while starting out financially. They end up coming back to their parents for money frequently after they move out, because they carry on like this, even when they cannot afford it. The sensible children understand that they can choose to walk, take the bus, make packed lunches, stay with friends/family or use budget hotels to save money, while they are trying to get on their feet. Wisdom is being intentional about teaching children that other options exist, even when we can afford to give them the best. There is a lot we can teach our children by ourselves (even in the younger years), if we are not keeping them in other people's care or in front of screens for most of the time. Kindness, healthy self esteem and a good work ethic are more important than getting straight As and speaking Queen's English. Being wise and intentional with our work schedules and finances helps us to make time for priceless, teachable moments, to save ourselves stress in the future.

It is also wise to work hard in your prime towards having more than one source of income, if you can. Africans are particularly doing well in the area of small business start-ups, in spite of the challenges. In countries like Nigeria, Ghana and Zambia, the number of women starting businesses outweighs men - probably because of employment challenges, the need for flexible working hours and extra income to support children's education. You do not need to wait until you have large amounts of capital to start a business, and you certainly do not need to give up your day job initially. This could mean some late nights and/or early mornings, but the investment could pay off, allowing you to have multiple income streams and more time for yourself eventually. If it is an idea you are passionate about, it will be a joy to work on it, even if you have to do it around a paid job. The important thing is to look after your mental health while in this phase and avoid prolonged periods of sleep deprivation and stress. Owning your own business is not an easy way out. It is hard work, but can be very rewarding. The virtuous woman in Proverbs 31 was described as hardworking, generous and honourable. It is difficult to be generous when you do not have enough for your own basic needs, so dream big.

Wisdom is about using money and loving people, not the other way round. When we genuinely care about people around us, instead of focusing so much on money, we can make great connections that save us money in future. Some people have to pay for care homes and taxis to hospital in old age because they have not a single friend or family member to help them! Having good social connections also helps us to get information and share money-saving ideas. For example, the timing of a purchase can save you money if you knew that there would be a discount offer during a specific period. Some people love bargains and like to take advantage of sales/discounts. Wisdom is realising that you save 100% by not buying things you do not need, which is better than saving 50% when you buy something you don't need in a half price sale. Money should be a tool to help us achieve things, and should be managed with wisdom. If you need to borrow money, it is wise to check for the best interest rates and review your repayments regularly. It might be worth setting up or changing your direct debit or standing order dates to days of the month that will be less stressful for you financially, depending on your paydays etc. Keeping your head in the sand when it comes to money/debt is not helpful for your mental health. You actually feel better when you take control and try to understand what you have to do. Just like we make ourselves shower and brush our teeth daily, even when we don't feel like it, because we know we will look and feel better afterwards; there are things that only you can do for yourself when it comes to managing your finances and creating a less stressful life. Getting organised is a simple thing that many ignore, but can completely change our lives and opportunities. Some people miss job interviews, business opportunities and important connections because they are too disorganised in their lives to plan ahead and get to places. The impact of poor organisation might also cost them money that they do not even have, through things like parking fines, speeding tickets, late payment charges and medical bills.

I have tried not to get too heavy on statistics in this book, partly because statistics often means nothing for the individual. Even if 99% of people from your background have bad outcomes, there is still hope that you can be in the 1% with a good outcome for your mental health and finances if you make some positive changes and good choices going forward. The first step to solving a problem is realising that we have one. It is wise to have a support system especially when sorting out your finances - people that understand what you are trying to achieve and wish you well. We might have people we love who will unfortunately hold on to beliefs and habits that are not helpful to their mental health or finances, but learning to manage such relationships is part of our growth as human beings. We are all different, but we can live peacefully when we respect the differences and set up healthy boundaries through sensitive communication. Avoid getting into financial traps like guaranteeing debt for others or committing to ongoing payments or "help" you really cannot afford. When we are intentional about our finances and time, we will start to see results in other aspects of our lives.

5.5 - A.H.A. (Afford, Help, Advance)

I did an online survey of 455 people from different parts of the world in December 2021 and January 2022 which showed that 87% thought that having or not having money affects their mental health and happiness. Almost all the participants (96%) felt that how we spend our days (e.g. our jobs or daily routine) has an effect on our mental health and life satisfaction. This is why this book is not just about money, but also about how we make money. In spite of this common knowledge, only 76% said that they would be interested in finding out more about the relationship between work/money and mental health, although about 91% said that they would be willing to change their lifestyle and attitude to work/money if they understood more about how these changes could improve their mental health and happiness. The big gap here suggests that people want a better life, but not all are willing to make the effort to *learn* how to get there. No one is born with "money sense" - it is all learned. If there is a specific area of finances we feel less confident about, there are ways to learn and improve. Books, videos and podcasts on the internet make it easier to access information these days, but not everyone is willing to make the effort. It is often said that "experience is the best teacher", but a wise person can learn from other people's experience without having to personally experience pain and loss. Thankfully, at the end of the year 2021 when most people were spending so much on Christmas celebrations, taxes, travel, etc, with some struggling due to winter blues and even seasonal affective disorder, and an ongoing pandemic, about 83% of participants in this survey said that they would describe their mental health as "generally good". There could be some bias here because those who were feeling low or unwell would probably have been less likely to take part in the survey, and even less likely to read books like this. Unfortunately, this is another way by which "the rich get richer and the poor get poorer", when people do not feel motivated or strong enough to access information and support to help them improve their circumstances. We can help such people around us by sharing information and encouraging them to make changes when they are ready. Reducing money stress and looking after our mental health is mainly about building good habits and being intentional with our finances.

Before making any significant financial decision, **think Aha!** This is a short way of remembering the important points below and looking after your mental wellbeing in this area. The definition of a significant financial decision will be different for us all and personal to you. While someone considers spending over ten million pounds their significant financial decision, someone else will consider £100 a lot of money. It is also important to note that little amounts also add up to significant amounts when we look at the bigger picture of our finances. Someone spending £20 a week on lunch at work could be spending around £1000 a year, which can be saved by eating leftovers from home dinners. Someone buying one small designer bag a month could be spending around £25,000 a year on this. For every significant expense, it is worth asking yourself the Aha! questions below.

AFFORD - **Can I afford this?** Be true to yourself and consider if you can really afford it after saving, paying your important bills and managing other expenses. Are you having to borrow money for it, or are you spending your own cash? If borrowing, is it an asset or a liability? If borrowing, is it a good interest rate, or can you get a better deal elsewhere? It is okay to not be able to afford something. You can always reconsider it in future after saving more money, or think of other ways to achieve the same aim. If the aim is to look nice for a party, you do not have to wear designer clothes to achieve that aim. If the aim is to live near a preferred school, you do not have to get the biggest house in the neighbourhood. We are often able to find other alternatives when we think of the "Why?". You do not have to beg, borrow or steal, because each option involves losing your pride, freedom or integrity. If it is really important, and you do not have the money, you might not mind asking friends/family to help if they can, but causing them stress should be a last resort, because everyone has their own needs and bills. There are also charities and crowdfunding websites that you might consider. Fraud/stealing is illegal and should not be an option. The guilty conscience, mental and legal problems that come with this option are not worth the trouble. This question helps to prevent unnecessary debt and stress which is not good for our mental health. If you can sensibly afford what you want, that's great! We can move on to the next point.

HELP - **Will it help?** This is not just a question about whether the purchase/spend will help you, but think about others also. No man is an island. Many wealthy people have found over the years that money really does not buy happiness, because there is no happiness in selfishness. Sometimes the money we wish to spend might literally be to help someone out of a difficult situation. As discussed above, we really need to consider if we are helping them or encouraging their dependence/laziness. It might be hard to say no, but that is sometimes the most helpful thing you can do in some situations. It is also important to think about if the spend will actually help you.

We sometimes spend a lot of money without thinking of the aim. Buying fatty takeaways every night does not actually help my weight and cholesterol level, but might help occasionally to reduce the "stress" of cooking for one night. It is about weighing the pros and cons when we make such decisions. This is where spending on unhealthy habits (e.g. smoking, drugs, alcohol excess) and entitled relatives/friends can be curbed.

ADVANCE - Finally, **does it advance my life's vision/ goal/purpose?** Some spending habits might seem harmless at first but when scrutinised in the context of your long term goals, they can be considered a waste of money. It does not make sense for me to spend so much money on depreciating items when my long term goal is to save capital for a business and/or to leave a sizable inheritance for my grandchildren. Spending so much money regularly on transportation to somewhere that adds no value to my life and goals will certainly be considered unwise in this section. This is a very personal question, and we can all answer "Yes" for anything we really want, but it works best when we are honest with ourselves and prioritise the things that really matter to us and help us. Some things are priceless and cannot be quantified in terms of money or gain. If I truly feel that the expensive trips I take with my children are what I need to advance my goal of having a good relationship with them and enjoy good mental health, so be it, as long as I can genuinely afford it, and it helps them too. It would not be helpful if I was regularly taking loans for this or taking them away in term time, for example. This point helps us to keep an eye on the bigger picture so we can have life satisfaction.

It has been an interesting experience reflecting and writing this book, because I am learning everyday too. I hope that it has given you a lot of food for thought, and helps us all to make changes that will give us better financial and health outcomes.

Personal Action Points

Other books
by Dr Afiniki Akanet

(all available on Amazon.co.uk and Afiniki.co.uk)

- 2020 Year of Plenty
- Taking CSA Tomorrow
- Life Without Coffee
  (Choosing Happiness Over Stress)
- Felicity
- Fortitude (The Story of a Nigerian Girl in the UK)

Resources and references

- https://www.who.int/news-room/fact-sheets/detail/mental-health-strengthening-our-response
- https://www.bbc.co.uk/news/health-27796628
- http://clok.uclan.ac.uk/31286/1/31286.pdf
- https://www.cambridge.org/core/journals/advances-in-psychiatric-treatment/article/psychiatric-and-psychological-aspects-of-fraud-offending/1B192F7E3AE4BAA1ED9BF1BFEA8F7063
- https://www.mind.org.uk/information-support/tips-for-everyday-living/money-and-mental-health/getting-support/
- https://www.afiniki.co.uk/blog
- https://www.mentalhealthandmoneyadvice.org/en/
- https://www.health.org.uk/publications/long-reads/unemployment-and-mental-health
- https://www.moneyandmentalhealth.org/press-release/vulnerable-people-online-scams/
- https://www.sciencedirect.com/science/article/abs/pii/S1057740813001149
- https://www.emerald.com/insight/content/doi/10.1108/YC-10-2018-0867/full/html

- https://www.mayoclinicproceedings.org/article/S0025-6196(11)62799-7/pdf
- https://www.forbes.com/sites/nicolefisher/2019/03/29/science-says-religion-is-good-for-your-health/?sh=581c3d9d3a12
- https://theconversation.com/the-forgotten-psychological-cost-of-corruption-in-developing-countries-156413
- https://www.mind.org.uk/information-support/guides-to-support-and-services/insurance-cover-and-mental-health/your-insurance-rights/
- https://www.local.gov.uk/sites/default/files/documents/tackling-poor-oral-health-d84.pdf
- https://www.nhs.uk/conditions/dementia/dementia-prevention/
- https://warwick.ac.uk/newsandevents/pressreleases/new_study_shows/
- https://www.experian.co.uk/consumer/guides/financial-association.html
- https://www.ons.gov.uk/peoplepopulationandcommunity/birthsdeathsandmarriages/divorce/bulletins/divorcesinenglandandwales/2019
- https://www.bbc.co.uk/news/business-42598969
- https://www.gov.uk/married-couples-allowance

- https://www.investopedia.com/articles/pf/09/marriage-killing-money-issues.asp#citation-2
- https://www.fool.com/investing/how-to-invest/cash-is-king/
- https://www.rcpsych.ac.uk/mental-health/problems-disorders/debt-and-mental-health#:~:text=One%20in%20two%20adults%20with,%2C%20depressed%20%E2%80%93%20or%20even%20hopeless
- https://journals.sagepub.com/doi/pdf/10.1177/1042258719837987
- https://www.mentalhealthandmoneyadvice.org/en/managing-money/how-are-mental-health-and-money-worries-linked/money-worries-and-mental-health/
- http://edition.cnn.com/2014/05/13/business/numbers-showing-africa-entrepreneurial-spirit/index.html
- http://web.mit.edu/jywang/www/cef/Bible/NIV/NIV_Bible/PROV+31.html
- https://www.gamcare.org.uk/get-support/talk-to-us-now/